CULTURE
.COM

Amanda —
It's all about the people!

Bob Stringh

PRAISE FOR
CULTURE.COM: HOW THE BEST STARTUPS MAKE IT HAPPEN

"Working with startups all over the world, I am thoroughly convinced that culture is the single most important factor determining success or failure of a startup. Bob Stringer's book is thus at the heart of making any startup a winner."

—Steven Koltai, Managing Director, Koltai & Company, LLC, and visiting scholar, Brookings Institution

"*Culture.com* is a must-read book for every early-stage entrepreneur. Adopting Stringer's seven dimensions of successful startup cultures is insanely important and, in my opinion, would make the difference between being a winner on paper and building a stronger successful startup."

—Erez Nahom, CEO & Cofounder of KonnecTo Top Tech Ltd.

"Startup culture is such a hot topic right now, and for good reason. *Culture.com* provides a set of tools and frameworks for creating and sustaining the right culture for your startup. As an educator, this book is a valuable resource to use in building up the softer skill set for entrepreneurs by using anecdotes and advice from successful founders to bring these challenges to life in an understandable way."

—Debi Kleiman, Executive Director, Blank Center for Entrepreneurship at Babson College

"You just can't underestimate the power of a winning culture—in both startups and larger organizations. I wish that I'd had Stringer's *Culture.com* when I was running companies. It is a must-read book for anyone trying to build an innovative, fast-growth organization."

—*Alex "Pete" Hart, Former CEO, Mastercard; Former Chair, Silicon Valley Bank; Chair, VeriFone Systems, Inc., director on numerous boards*

"As a former entrepreneur and a now a VC, I am acutely aware of the importance of culture as a determinant of the success of startups. Especially here in the Bay Area, in the first stage of life for startups, it's all about product. Before too long, culture—which seemed like a soft subject—becomes more important than all the rest. *Culture.com* is an invaluable guide for anyone trying to build a winning enterprise."

—*Ron Croen, Partner, Youandmrjones.com, Founder and former CEO, Nuance*

"In *Culture.com*, Bob Stringer perfectly captures the why, what, and how of creating a high-performing culture—the secret weapon of any really successful startup. Compelling, well researched, and thoroughly convincing, *Culture.com* is a must read for any startup leader who wants to build something great."

—*Chris Colbert, Managing Director, Harvard Innovation Labs*

"In our experience with thousands of MassChallenge startups, we have found entrepreneurs always hungry for practical advice about how to build a winning culture. *Culture.com* addresses this head-on. It will be an invaluable resource for the early-stage companies we work with around the world."

—*John Harthorne, CEO, MassChallenge*

"With over 50 years of research based findings and extensive interviews with the leadership of over 100 startups, Bob Stringer has provided us with a guidebook that moves way beyond the simple anecdotes that pervade the literature and the startup conference circuit. If there is time to read only one book this is it! Don't miss out!"

—Len Schlesinger, Baker Foundation Professor-Harvard Business School; President Emeritus-Babson College

"I've been on the founding team of three startups. I sure wish that I'd have read Stringer's book, *Culture.com: How the Best Startups Make it Happen*, seven years ago. It would have helped me and my co-founders navigate all of the people aspects of building our technology businesses. It is a quick and engaging read that founding teams will find invaluable."

—Havell Rodriques, CEO and Co-founder, Adjoint Inc

From our early days to the time that Constant Contact went public, culture was a critical driver of our success. Who better to write about culture than Bob Stringer, who has been studying this for over 40 years? Reading the book is a great opportunity for people in startups to learn from the guru.

—Gail Goodman, Former CEO, Constant Contact

CULTURE
.COM

HOW THE
BEST STARTUPS
MAKE IT HAPPEN

ROBERT STRINGER

Crimson Seed Capital Publishing

CULTURE.com: How the Best Startups Make It Happen

Copyright © 2017 by Robert Stringer

All Rights Reserved

Published by Crimson Seed Capital Publishing
Boston, MA
www.crimsonseedcapital.com

For information, see www.culturedotcom.com

First Edition

Independent publishing support by Gatekeeper Press

Library of Congress Cataloging-in-Publication Data has been applied for.

ISBN: 978-0-692-96264-0 (hardcover)
ISBN: 978-0-692-05364-5 (softcover)
ISBN: 978-1-5323-5768-8 (ebook)

A Note on
Interviews and Kate Merritt

Kate Merritt assisted the author in conducting many of the interviews that form the basis of much of the research that went into this book. She also contributed significantly to the book's content and wrote Appendix B-2 (Culture Assessment). The author owns all the quotes, comments, and endorsements, and each person interviewed was aware of our purpose and intention to use their quotes or endorsements in this book.

To Diane, who is almost as good an entrepreneur
as she is a wife.

About the Author

Robert Stringer is an active angel investor in startups, and a board member of and advisor to early-stage companies in five countries. His portfolio of over 30 ventures has given him a unique perspective on what it takes to succeed in today's ultracompetitive business world. Previously, he was a venture capitalist (he founded Sherbrooke Capital, a $100 million health-and-wellness fund), a business-school professor at the Harvard Business School and at Babson's Olin School of Business, and the author of three popular books on culture and business strategy.

His first book, *Motivation and Organizational Climate*, coauthored with George Litwin, won the McKinsey award for the best book in management. Robert has also published a book on business strategy (*Strategy Traps and How to Avoid Them*), and one on culture and leadership (*Leadership and Organizational Climate*). In all of these publications, Bob has focused on the relationship between leadership, motivation, and culture.

Contact information:

Bob@culturedotcom.com
@RAStringer
www.linkedin.com/in/bob-stringer

Contents

Introduction

WHEN ENTREPRENEURS SEEK expert advice to help them put together a compelling business plan, they turn to product gurus, technology experts, and folks with sales and marketing, fundraising, operations, or finance backgrounds. But for guidance on how to create a high-performance company culture—the softer side of startup strategy—rarely will entrepreneurs find a source of advice and counsel. *Culture.com: How the Best Startups Make It Happen*, a research-based exploration of what it takes to build and sustain a winning startup culture, fills that void.

My personal insight into startup cultures began when I was at the Harvard Business School (HBS). One of my professors, George Litwin, was deeply involved with research into achievement motivation—the basic social motive behind risk-taking and entrepreneurial behavior. The laboratory experiments that George and I conducted at Harvard demonstrated conclusively that startup cultures (a) could be created in a very short period of time—a matter of weeks in our study; (b) that these cultures aroused the achievement motivation of the members of the startup; and (c) that, once aroused, these high-achieving cultures outperformed similar organizations competing in the same industry. George and I wrote a book about this research called *Motivation and Organizational Climate*, which won the McKinsey award for the Best Book in Management in 1968.

The implications of this research have largely been ignored, partly because startups were not a hot topic until the 1990s and the rise of dotcoms. But, I believe that one of the most powerful dynamics behind the rapid growth and success of the best startups is their high-achieving cultures. (The role of achievement motivation is explained in greater detail in Chapter 2 and in Appendix A.)

Culture.com: How the Best Startups Make It Happen is more than one person's impressions of what cool startup cultures feel like and how they work. It relies on a series of empirical research initiatives focused on the social and motivational dynamics of young, early-stage businesses (companies that have existed for fewer than five years and that employ between 10 and 100 people), and combines the motivational research on culture that George and I conducted at Harvard with extensive interview research that I conducted in 2017 with over 100 startups. In addition to describing the HBS research, Appendix A provides more detail on the book's research foundations. Other appendices provide readers with practical diagnostic and culture management tools, as well as samples of some culture statements from the best and most successful startups.

Understanding and thoughtfully managing the softer side of a startup's strategy should be vitally important to every entrepreneur. Research and experience also highlights its importance to other players in the entrepreneurial ecosystem, including startup advisors, incubators, board members, and investors in early-stage companies. As a former venture capitalist, I know all about the perils of ignoring a company's culture. Here is a true story, which starts with an extremely uncomfortable conversation:

Monday, 10:35 a.m.

John Heuser, managing general partner of Venture Capital Partners, LLC (VCP), wasn't happy. And when John was unhappy, Andy Hunter, the general partner for early stage investments at VCP was miserable.

"What the hell happened in the last 60 days over at DataBracket? I thought we were all set for a B round and cruising toward a possible liquidation event late next year. Now

VCP will have to fly solo if we try to raise more capital. And your voice mail last night said we might be looking at a total write-off." John was obviously having a hard time controlling his anger and disappointment.

"Well, uh, what can I say? It's a real mess at DataBracket, and I just didn't see it coming. John . . . this is on me . . ."

"I'll say it is. It's your *job* to stay ahead of things like this. That's why you were on the DB board—you were supposed to be our eyes and ears there. For Pete's sake, Andy, you were the enthusiastic sponsor of this deal." John reached for his tonic water and took a series of deep breaths. "Tell me what happened. The last time we looked at the DB numbers, almost everything was trending in the right direction. You said Brandon [Kelly, the founder and CEO of DataBracket] was doing an okay job over there."

Andy looked away. "I really thought he was, but I guess I was wrong. Last month we lost two pretty important engineers— you remember I was pretty concerned about that. But Brandon went into a big song and dance about how they were 'not his kind of people,' and that he had two 'great replacements' in the wings. As I told you last night, they both quit last Friday."

"Andy, let me get this straight. Wasn't DB's engineering talent supposed to be a big part of its success formula? Hell, that's why we put almost a million bucks into the damn company . . ."

"I know. I know. I'm due to meet Brandon this afternoon. I will get to the bottom of this."

Monday, 5:45 p.m.

Andy pushed his chair back from the conference table, and leafed through the five pages of notes that he'd just taken from his meeting with the DataBracket (DB) engineers and support staff. Talk about a leadership failure. He'd heard nothing but complaints and disillusionment from the employees who were supposed to be the backbone of a high-flying software startup.

As soon as he'd asked Brandon to leave the room, the dam broke. What a sweatshop the place seemed to be. The distraught venture capitalist (VC) now realized how badly he'd misjudged the situation at DB. He should have had this afternoon's meeting 10 months ago. He should have dug a lot deeper into what was going on behind the scenes.

He should have paid a lot more attention to the soft stuff.

Earlier in the afternoon, his discussion with Brandon had gone poorly. He admitted that although the basic DB burn rate was according to plan, two of the company's largest customers had recently found major bugs in the software they'd purchased and had insisted on costly re-dos. Progress payments were being withheld, and there was talk of renegotiating both customers' annual contracts. Brandon had showed Andy what he called his "plan B cash flow projection" and it was ugly.

Andy also learned that the CFO, Will Brant, and Charlie Argenti, DB's co-founder and technical guru, had had several loud—and very public—arguments about cost overruns and unplanned charges to fix the quality problems with the software. Although Andy and the other two outside board members had never been especially happy with the high level financial summaries they received from Will, he was viewed as competent . . . and certainly not a hothead. Evidently, the latest shouting match had taken place two days ago. Charlie had been holed up in his office ever since and Will had been overheard commiserating with his team about the "losers" in development. It was that revelation that led Andy to insist on a spur of the moment confidential meeting with a hastily gathered group of DB employees.

Tuesday, 3:00 p.m.

Andy had spent the night and most of the morning reviewing his notes and impressions, collecting his thoughts, and writing up his analysis of the DB situation. John had called a partners meeting and DB was the only item on the agenda.

Although Andy was no novice when it came to investing in startups and knew that John and his fellow partners could stomach the bad news, he felt obligated to summarize what he called "the lessons learned."

Here's part of what Andy planned to say:

> The most important lesson we have to learn from our DB experience is that culture trumps strategy, great products, and even market acceptance. DataBracket was a clear winner on paper. It had the right technology, the right go-to-market strategy, and the right customers. What it didn't have was the right culture.
>
> Brandon hired the best and the brightest 24 months ago, but he never figured out how to manage and motivate his technical talent, his sales force, or his customer support people. That was 80 percent of the company. He tried to direct and control it all. He spent most of his time promoting DB to the outside world. Brandon was 'Mr. Outside,' but he also tried to be 'Mr. Inside.' And Charlie was no better when it came to the people and the culture. They had both ignored the early signs of discomfort, discontent, and poor morale, and Brandon, Will, and Charlie were simply tone-deaf when it came to that side of the business. All they cared about was top-line growth and sending us the good-news numbers.
>
> "I'm hoping that the situation is fixable, but not with the current senior team. The DB culture is the product of two years of non-leadership and mismanagement. Shame on us—and on me—for not recognizing how critical the company's culture can be when it comes to the success of a startup.

Being tone-deaf to the soft side of a business has long been recognized as a fatal leadership flaw in large organizations. But it's increasingly clear that it is also a fatal flaw for leaders of younger startup companies. And it's so much easier to build a winning culture in the beginning, than it is to try a fix a culture that's gone bad.

What Is Culture?

What exactly is Andy talking about when he refers to the company's culture, and is there any way to change it?

If you look up the term *corporate culture* on Amazon, you get some 40 million hits, and there are certainly hundreds of different definitions for culture to be found in all of those publications. Not surprisingly, through the years there has been no single definition of culture that everyone agrees with. Some of the definitions emphasize what people do. For example, Boston Consulting Group defines culture as " . . . a characteristic set of behaviors that define how things get done in an organization."[1] Others define it in more academic terms and focus on what people think or feel. Culture guru Edgar Schein talks about culture " . . . as systems of shared meanings, assumptions, and underlying values."[2] Ben Schneider, another well-known culture expert, writes that " . . . culture is a common set of shared meanings or understandings about the group/organization and its problems, goals, and practices."[3]

For my purposes I'll keep the definition simple: An organization's culture is what the members of the organization experience. We don't have to parse people's experience into what's a norm, what's a value, what's an unwritten rule, or what's an assumption or tradition. Therefore, we can define cultures—and in this book, startup cultures— by interviewing the members of an organization and asking them to describe their experience: what it feels like to work there and what impact those feelings have on their motivation and behavior.

Perhaps another simple way to think about the cultural attributes of startups is a comment from Ron Croen, an experienced Bay Area VC and former entrepreneur: "People have values and organizations have cultures."

What Is a Startup?

This is an easier task. Depending on the nature of the business, top-line revenue and the number of employees or years in existence are all possible variables to consider when determining what a startup is. The formative months and years of a company's culture, and how that culture was (or was not) scaled as the company grew are two areas not studied much to date, and therefore the research underlying this book examined young, early stage businesses—startups that had between 10 and 100 employees and that were in existence less than five years. Defining a startup simply based on the company's revenues is an issue because industry economics vary significantly and a successful level of revenue in some industries is defined with lots of zeros, and in other industries, with a lot fewer.

What You Will Learn

This book is aimed at prospective entrepreneurs (especially those who have never started a business), investors, advisors, and board members of startup companies, members of management teams of struggling early-stage companies, and academics and consultants who teach entrepreneurship or coach entrepreneurial leaders. All the research confirms that culture is a critical component of a startup's ultimate success. A company's culture starts on day one, and personal leadership is the primary determinant of that culture. As the startup begins to scale—especially if the growth is explosive, as many high-tech ventures are—there will be many cultural obstacles to be faced by entrepreneurial leaders. But these can be overcome if leaders have better insight and the right tools at their disposal. *Culture.com: How the Best Startups Make it Happen* provides them.

CHAPTER 1

The Importance of Culture

THE IMPORTANCE OF a company's culture has long been recognized in academic and business circles. The importance of culture in startup organizations, however, has tended to be ignored due to the myriad of other factors that startups always have to deal with. This unfortunate fact has been around for a long time, in spite of the laboratory research conducted at the Harvard Business School that proved that achievement motivation—perhaps the most significant source of entrepreneurial activity—was aroused and reinforced by a company's work environment. (See Appendix A for a description of this research.)

But the vast majority of entrepreneurs included in the 2017 research sample state that their company's culture is a significant source of competitive advantage. Interviewees emphasized this point many times in quotes like "Culture eats strategy for breakfast"; "Culture beats strategy"; and "If I had to bet on a great product or a great culture, I'd bet on culture."

These statements are not new. Multiple business experts have invented such phrases but the bottom line is that a lot of people have finally recognized the value of having the right kind of culture when it comes to driving early-stage business success.

All the interviews of Boston-based startups reinforce this conclusion. Tom Dretler, founder and CEO of Shorelight Education, says, "Shorelight's culture was and is today a critical engine of growth." Ellen Rubin, CEO of ClearSky Data, echoes Dretler's perspective: "This is my third startup and, to me and my cofounder, culture matters as much or more than our product, our marketing prowess, or our business strategy." Stefania Mallett, founder of ezCater, agrees: "Culture is king."

Dretler, Rubin, and Mallett are experienced founders and they've obviously learned many lessons about the importance of culture over the course of building multiple startups. But even first-time founders like Rob Biederman of Catalant Technologies are convinced of the critical impact of culture. Biederman even moved the location of his startup because of the culture: "We moved out of our incubator space primarily because we couldn't have the right kind of culture there."

Why is culture so important to startup founders and CEOs? There are at least six reasons, and for most entrepreneurs more than one of them is always in play.

1. Culture is one of the clearest reflections of the quality of your offer to customers. Entrepreneurs—especially dotcom entrepreneurs with a sexy technology—often rely too much on the technical functionality of their product when it comes to communicating the value of their offer. But the customer experience is what tends to define the true quality of a company's product or service. Startup leaders come to realize that it's their job to motivate their people to deliver experiences that signal the highest levels of overall quality. In addition to getting all the bugs out of their software, this means paying close attention to culture.

   When Diane Hessan was CEO of Communispace, her startup's culture emphasized that responding to customer needs was one of the main components of the company's quality reputation: "We took great pride in our responsiveness, even working through the weekends to solve a customer's problem. In our industry, our culture was more important than our software when it came to defining the quality and value of our product."

The absence of the right kind of culture very often is at the heart of a lousy quality reputation. Just ask Anthony Rodio, president and CEO of Your Mechanic, a Mountain View startup that sends mechanics to fix your car whenever you need it and wherever your car may be. Rodio took over the leadership of Your Mechanic after the founders had created what he labels "a toxic tops-down culture," which had ruined the company's image for quality service. For example, missed service calls, ignoring customer complaints, and a general "we don't care about you" attitude were all too common. Rodio is working hard to change the culture to improve the perception of the quality of Your Mechanic's offer.

2. Culture functions as the flip side of the company's brand. Closely related to signaling quality, culture plays a broader role in communicating the priorities and values of the business. Tony Hsieh, founder of Zappos, makes this point over and over again when he talks about building his company into an ecommerce powerhouse. Founders who pour millions of dollars into marketing programs to externally tout their breakthrough technology need to also make sure that the brand values and brand promises resonate internally. And this requires paying a lot of attention to the company's culture. For startups, this imperative begins as soon as the products and services are in the market. Gail Goodman, CEO of Constant Contact (CC), reflects: "Our culture was always on my mind; and it was always a priority." CC's mission of helping small businesses harness the power of ecommerce and the Internet required, according to Gail, a fixation on serving the evolving needs of their customers. And this, in turn, required a work environment that was responsive,

cooperative, and compassionate. "From the beginning, " Goodman says, "we wanted the right kind of culture to match our brand. This meant that everyone who touched our customers had to have the right attitude. So we adopted a 'no-assholes' policy to minimize any doubts about our cultural norms."

3. Culture is a critical tool for attracting and retaining talent. The importance of having the right kind of culture to the founders of startups in the Bay Area cannot be overestimated. Without exception, culture was called out as a critical source of competitive advantage when it came to hiring and retaining talent. Conor Begley, founder and president of Tribe Dynamics, confirms that his company's culture was one of the strongest incentives for attracting engineering talent. So does Greg Golub, founder and CEO of Sequoia. Mike Tamir, one of the earliest hires at Takt, cites a study that says the average tenure of a high quality engineer in the Bay Area is only a short 1.1 years. He emphasizes that the Takt culture seeks to beat this statistic by stressing high levels of personal responsibility, risk-taking, innovation, and feedback. In a world where your engineers are getting calls from headhunters every week, it's no wonder startups try to focus on having the kind of high-achieving, innovation-driven cultures that engineers prefer.

4. The right kind of culture allows startups to adjust their strategies, pivot, innovate, and rebound from adversity. When entrepreneurs say that *culture beats strategy* that is what they mean. Almost all of the most successful entrepreneurs admit that they and their companies have had to execute strategic pivots—sometimes, dramatic ones that changed the originally conceived business model. "It was one thing for me, the CEO, to recognize

when things were going off the rails and we needed to change our strategy. But the key to our success was having people and a culture that were open to change and flexible enough to actually embrace the new direction." This comment comes from Franco Capurro, founder and CEO of Caaapital S.p.A., a Latin American fintech startup, and it is a theme heard over and over again in the research interviews. Two of the most important aspects of successful startup cultures are openness and a willingness to learn by doing. In the beginning, when a founder's ideas are still being tested, it is important to have others in the organization who are motivated to experiment, poke holes, and try out new approaches without fearing criticism about not getting on board with a potentially flawed product or program.

5. A startup's culture makes a statement about the founder's values. Many entrepreneurs, especially those who have started more than one company, explicitly state that they aimed to build a culture that reflected their own values and priorities. Joshua Summers, founder and CEO of clypd (his third startup), speaks for many founders when he says: "My cofounder and I wanted to build a great company with a great culture. That was really our top priority. After that, we decided upon clypd's actual product." Bettina Hein, CEO of Pixability (her second startup) echoes this same thought: "My goal was to create a certain kind of company with a culture that was built around my values and principles."

6. The right kind of culture motivates extraordinary commitment and effort. To be successful, a startup requires a tremendous amount of hard work—not only from the founders, but also from everyone in the company. Several entrepreneurs admit that in the beginning, employees are

sometimes expected to sleep under their desks. They do it and they love doing it. How can this be? There are as many answers to this question as there are individuals working in startups. But a few main motivators predominate:

a. It is viewed as a small price for employees to pay for doing what they love. And what they love is working on exciting projects, doing work that might change the world, being fully responsible for a deliverable without lots of second-guessing or supervision, and working alongside—and being supported by—a group of talented colleagues.

b. As is summarized in Appendix A, certain kinds of cultures arouse an individual's need for achievement, which is a powerful intrinsic motive that many startup employees possess. Most, if not all, successful startups have high-achieving cultures, i.e., cultures that "turn on" the need for achievement.

c. Another major incentive is the ability to have a direct, individual impact on the business; employees want to be the people building the basic processes and systems underlying the work rather than having to blindly follow established procedures.

d. For many people, being part of a new wave of technology is a big driver. They want to work for a cutting-edge startup where they can be exposed to new ideas and learn new approaches that make them more employable and more valuable.

e. Financial incentives, while not a dominant motivator, certainly play a major role. Why not pull a few all-nighters if your options might triple in value if the software works better?

The only startup entrepreneurs who do not say that culture mattered that much are those who are first-time founders with fewer than 10 employees. Founders such as Mike Brungardt of Pro Hoop Strength, Adam O'Neal, founder of Broga, and Kaan Aykac, founder of Gezlong, all focused almost exclusively on perfecting their technology, acquiring customers, and raising capital. It would be a real tragedy if these entrepreneurs were successful in these efforts only to see their companies go the way of DataBracket and thousands of other technology-enabled startups. The research shows that even in the earliest stages of a startup's existence, culture matters.

CHAPTER 2

The Right Kind of Startup Culture

THERE IS ALMOST universal agreement among the entrepreneurs who were interviewed that the culture in a startup matters a lot. There is also substantial agreement on a set of concepts that describe the right kind of startup culture. The specific words vary a lot, but the underlying ideas were very consistent.

The differences involve the question of which aspects of culture contribute the most to the success of these fledgling businesses. These differences are in emphasis, not in substance. Nuances depend on four factors or "realities" that these entrepreneurs experience. The right kind of culture

- has to fit and respond to the competitive situation, particularly as it relates to acquiring and satisfying customers and attracting and retaining talent;

- has to fit with employees' expectations and aspirations, especially the needs of the earliest members of the startup team;

- has to fit with the emerging business strategy—most pointedly, the company's ability to adjust to new opportunities and recover from mistakes; and

- has to fit with the founder's values and the founding team's willingness and ability to demonstrate the kind of leadership that reinforces those values.

So, what is the right kind of startup culture? What are the things that the founders and CEOs of the most successful startups emphasize and that the members of their organizations experience? The following is a brief description of seven aspects or dimensions of culture that are the most important. The rest of this book will describe the dynamics of each dimension and provide entrepreneurs, startup advisors, and VCs with a to-do list of actions and practices that can be employed to create and reinforce the right kind of startup culture.

The 7 Dimensions of Successful Startup Cultures

Most startups fail. Successful startups—at least those that have survived and grown over the first five years of their existence—share the following cultural features. Not surprisingly, there are lots of overlaps, but entrepreneurs should treat each dimension as a startup-culture imperative.

1. Passion

   Winning cultures require *everyone* to be passionate about accomplishing the startup's basic mission. The founder and members of the top team must lead the way here, but their absolute commitment has to be contagious. As Peter Thiel writes in *Zero to One*, successful startups need to have "cultures of total dedication."[1] Canh Tran, CEO of Rippleshot, is passionate about improving financial security and preventing card fraud. The company's website states, "Our team is committed to our mission of making people feel secure about the financial information they're using, storing or transacting with." All the data scientists who work at Rippleshot share Tran's personal passion for this mission.

Passion about the mission is heightened when the company has a larger social purpose. Daniel Chao, founder and CEO of Halo Neuroscience, a startup that makes HaloSport, a neurostimulator that helps athletes train better, puts it this way: "Our business today is focused on athletes, and this is an exciting and fun target market. But it's our basic mission that motivates everyone here. Think of epilepsy. Our technology will ultimately serve as an important rehabilitation device. It's this vision that we all are committed to."

How do founders know if they have a culture where people are passionate about the mission? Employees feel proud. They feel excited to be contributing to a purpose higher than simply making a financial killing or working in a cool place. They are motivated to go the extra mile, even if it sometimes means sleeping under their desks. And they are committed—not only to the mission, but also to their leaders and their colleagues.

2. Ownership

Winning startups are filled with people who are willing to do almost anything to make the business a success. For that to happen, people have to feel that they "own" the business and the work they do, that it's *their* money, *their* customers, and *their* success if the business thrives. As T.J. Mahony, CEO of FlipKey, defines it, "Ownership is like babysitting your own child as opposed to someone else's."

Ownership means taking the initiative. When employees feel like owners, they feel empowered to take action and make decisions without always waiting for someone to direct them, which is a big benefit when speed is important. Ownership means that the leadership team must let go. As Mahony emphasizes, "If you want ownership, then delegation has to start early. We had to tell the folks that worked for us, 'This is all yours.'"

When the founders consciously or unconsciously decide to own too much, the culture turns toxic. Melissa Footlick, COO of TopStepTrader, in Chicago, recalls the company's early days: "It was a command-and-control place, with the senior team in their ivory tower barking out orders. Letting employees have autonomy felt like too big a risk. So we were losing people left and right, and we couldn't get new people to join. It was a disaster." It was only after a dramatic nine-month intervention, led by The Junto Institute for Entrepreneurial Leadership, that the TopStepTrader senior team let go of some control and created a culture of broad-based Ownership.

3. Learning

Winning startup cultures are learning cultures. Unless a startup's founders are incredibly lucky, they don't hit on the best strategy, the best product, or the best use of their technology right out of the gate. Successful entrepreneurs observe what works, throw out what doesn't, and move on. It's learning by doing and it requires a culture that supports this often-frustrating kind of progress. Think of what it must feel like to be hired for your skills in ABC software, only to find out that XYZ software works better for customers and is what the company now wants to focus on. Unless the culture is absolutely dedicated to learning by doing, the best engineers will leave. Jon Radoff, CEO of Disruptor Beam, has built a high-learning culture at his startup gaming company. "I expect my people to think of themselves as learners, not knowers. We accept mistakes when they lead to new insights and ideas."

Successful founders work at making Learning both important and safe, for example, with lunch-and-learn sessions every week or regular development days on which people can flesh out their own product ideas and present the results to the whole company. A Learning culture requires that leaders be coaches. At FlipKey, Mahony's rule is, never let anyone do something for the first time without a more senior person along for guidance and support. Often, founders themselves have had mentors—other CEOs they could turn to for regular advice and feedback. In startups that succeed, everybody learns.

4. Collaboration

For successful startups, winning is a team sport. When you have limited resources, people have to help each other out to get things done. The first thing to do is to hire people who are team players. Constant Contact CEO Goodman states simply, "You couldn't work here unless you played well with others." Fred Shilmover, CEO of InsightSquared, puts it another way: "Because winning requires teamwork, it's hard to perform well here *and* be a jerk." Finding great collaborators who are also great engineers, developers, or data scientists can be a daunting task. This is why so many successful startups spend so much time vetting new employees. It is not uncommon for a successful startup to expect new hires to speak to 10 or more people before an offer is made. Because hiring young talent with untested collaboration skills, Ellen Rubin, founder of ClearSky Data, finds that paring them with older, more experienced software developers helps young talent become better collaborators.

But a collaborative culture requires more than hiring a bunch of team players (assuming you can weed out the jerks). The best startups create collaborative working spaces. Open-floor plans with few closed offices and employees, including the CEO, who sit next to one another makes collaboration easier. Recent research cited by Lindsey Kaufman in a *Washington Post* article, "Google Got it Wrong. The Open-Office Trend Is Destroying the

Workplace," disputes the contention that a completely open-floor plan promotes productivity.[2,3] Noise and distractions can bother employees who are used to having private offices. Shilmover has his own take on this issue: "No offices means good ideas win." Ellen Rubin explains that in her offices, she has several designated "gathering areas" designed and supplied with white boards. These spaces deliberately had no walls or doors, which meant that discussions could be overheard. The idea was to encourage anyone who had something to contribute to join the conversation and offer ideas. That's a culture of collaboration.

It's not enough to have collaboration within a team. In successful startups, you'll see collaboration across teams from different departments as well as across levels in the organization, with junior and senior people working easily together.

Hiring team players is a good start. Designing open conversation space is necessary. But people take their cues from the founder and the senior team. In winning cultures, leaders respect each other's opinions, back up each other's decisions, and keep their disagreements private.

5. Messiness

Successful startups are messy places. There are no written policies or procedures, formal rules or job descriptions. Many success stories include tales of overcrowded offices, of people without a desk to call their own, and of work getting done at all hours of the day and night. In a successful startup, messiness is not a problem; it is embraced. Rob Biederman of Catalant Technologies calls it "being scrappy." Messiness comes from trying to do more with less. It means doing lots of workarounds and finding creative ways to save time and money.

Why does this work? Founders should appreciate that a culture that embraces messiness is a culture of flexibility. It's a place where people focus more on getting the work done than on following step-by-step instructions or procedures. Yes, it can lead to mistakes. But it also leads to experimentation and innovation. It allows the business to pivot and to move with speed to take advantage of emerging market opportunities or new technology without having to dismantle formal processes and systems. In addition, a culture that tolerates Messiness can be much more fun than one that doesn't. That's why it works for so many high-tech engineers and Millennials.

6. Transparency

Winning startups value transparency. Both the good news and the bad news about the business are shared openly. The most effective startup CEOs and founders overcommunicate to make sure people know what's going on. At Pixability, Hein shares the company's cash position with her folks every month. Corey Thomas, Rapid7's CEO, organizes monthly town halls to discuss what's going on at all levels of the company. Communispace's Hessan not only held a staff meeting every Tuesday to go over all the numbers, she also sent a weekend voice-mail message—updates, congratulations, a heads-up for the coming week—to every employee in the company each weekend for 12 years.

Hessan tells a story that illustrates how valuable Transparency can be. In March 2001, the Internet bubble had imploded and Communispace had only four months of cash left. She called a company-wide staff meeting and shared all the disturbing facts and numbers. Then she asked people to work in small groups to come up with specific recommendations for what she and the senior team could do to turn things around. Hessan implemented most of these ideas and successfully got the business back on track. The culture of Transparency at Communispace was clearly a source of competitive advantage. Eleven years after that fateful meeting in 2001, the company was sold to Omnicom for a nice fat price.

When you experience a culture of Transparency, you quickly understand that honesty and openness is an important part of the company's success formula. Disruptor Beam's Radoff calls this cultural theme "authenticity." People at all levels are expected to speak their minds, call a spade a spade, and to have no patience for secrets, hidden agendas, or hypocrisy. That kind of honesty makes it easy to rally around the mission, pitch in to do the hard work, and share in the startup's success.

7. Caring

    Startup companies are demanding. Successful startups, however, have a caring and supportive culture. The pressure to perform—even the expectation that you will sleep under your desk when necessary—is coupled with a genuine sense of caring for the personal wellbeing of the members of the organization. Relationships count. People count. Several successful entrepreneurs describe earlier startups that failed precisely because they didn't pay enough attention to the importance of caring. Rippleshot's Tran makes this point: "People want to belong to a community, they want to be on a winning team. But they also want to be part of a team that cares about them as individuals."

    A culture of Caring isn't about having Ping-Pong tables, free food, and beer parties on Fridays (although these perks may send the right signals). Employees don't have to spend all of their off hours having fun with their colleagues to have a sense of a caring community. In a culture of Caring people feel valued and appreciated as individuals as well as contributors to the business. Joshua Summers, cofounder and CEO at clypd, shares an example: "A couple of summers ago, we had a man down—one of our interns had an accident and ended up in the hospital for over a month. Even though this guy was new and was actually a temporary hire, we kept him on the payroll the whole time. And folks from the company visited him every day." How do you think that resonated with the rest of the clypd team? A culture of Caring added to people's motivation to make clypd a success.

The best startups exhibit all—or almost all—of these seven cultural dimensions. However, they make it happen in unique ways that fit the four requirements listed at the beginning of this chapter. Although there is no single right kind of culture that works for every startup, there are at least five archetype cultures that have driven the success of companies in the research sample.

CHAPTER 3

Winning Cultural Archetypes

W HEN MOST PEOPLE think of a typical startup, they think of a CEO in a hoodie and a loft space with rows of open-desk areas surrounded by food, dogs, and Ping-Pong tables.

Some startup cultures are like this, but there are many that aren't. There are various types of startup cultures that lead to success. One useful way to think about the right kind of startup culture for your enterprise is to look at cultural archetypes. These archetype cultures display distinctive patterns of the seven dimensions of startup cultures described Chapter 2, and have proved to be the right kind of culture—at least for a while—for any number of startups. But none of the archetypes is in any way perfect. The right kind of culture for a given startup has to fit the competitive situation, the entrepreneur's values, the startup's strategy, and the personal motivations of the members of the organization. Would-be entrepreneurs should think about these factors as they review and evaluate the appropriateness of the five startup-culture archetypes described below. Following the description of each archetype is a diagnostic tool, or culture quiz, to use to help you decide which archetype may be right for your venture.

Archetype 1: The Customer-Obsessed Culture

There are successful startups that attribute their growth and profitability to their cultural obsession with overdelivering value to their customers. These startups win because they go beyond all expectations of good customer service or creating a positive customer experience. For these startups, customer obsession is a strategy to create uncommon loyalty, and barriers to entry that can be as formidable as a new technology breakthrough.

This kind of strategy is especially powerful for B2B companies, in which strong references are a critical component of the success formula and the business model relies on renewals, long-term subscriptions, and customers saying *yes* on a continuous basis.

Three companies in the research sample come immediately to mind: Communispace (now called C Space), the startup cited in Chapter 1 that invented private, online customer communities; ThinkCERCA, a literacy-platform startup that is trying to revolutionize the way students learn critical thinking; and Constant Contact, the company that focuses on making its small-business customers more successful marketers.

What is it like to work in a customer-obsessed startup culture? What makes this kind of culture so successful? What are the keys to having a customer-obsessed culture? What are the pitfalls and drawbacks of such a culture? When Apple decided to open retail stores, it already had a highly differentiated and successful product line. Its Apple Stores were, in a very real sense, startups. But Ron Johnson, who was the early head of Apple Stores, decided to win as a customer-obsessed enterprise. And he did. The level of service people received in those early Apple Stores astonished customers. Apple staff, one-to-one assistants, and Genius Bar experts were everywhere. It was an amazing customer experience and when you talked to Apple Store employees, it was an amazing experience for them, as well. They felt valued and special. They knew that they were breaking new ground in the technology retail world, and they were proud to be part of the Apple Store revolution.

Disney is another example of a large company with a customer-obsessed culture. Visit a Disney theme park and you will quickly realize that part of its success formula is to overstaff the customer-service function. No problem is too large, no question too dumb, and even the maintenance people are happy to give you directions to your next ride. There is always someone there with his or her name on a Disney badge, ready to help make your experience as close to perfect as possible.

What can other smaller, less well-known, and less wealthy startups learn from the Apple Store and Disney examples?

In customer-obsessed cultures, the most critical experience employees can have is to "walk around" in the customers' shoes. Walking around means much more than doing customer research or taking a good customer to lunch or inviting customers to help you brainstorm new product or service ideas. It means listening to customers and understanding them on a gut level. It means seeing customers as people, not market segments, and knowing exactly how they use your product, knowing what counts the most in the customer experience, and really understanding customers' hopes and fears. Most important, it means acting on this knowledge with alacrity and enthusiasm. It means making customers the heroes, telling their stories, and giving them the credit for your success.

One of the mottos that CC's Goodman drove home to her earliest employees—and emphasized for the 15 years that she ran CC—was simple, but profound: "We are not our customer." Listening hard to each small business's needs, learning what they value, what they want, what they hate, and how they live is what Goodman expected her people to do. All successful startups have to understand their customers, but not all go to the lengths that Goodman did. For example:

- CC's salespeople were called coaches, not salespeople. Coaches were committed to making their learners successful, not just selling them something.

- All of CC's weekly meetings began and ended with customer stories.

- After hurricane Katrina, CC gave all its affected customers six months of free service—they needed it to get back on their feet.

- When CC opened a call center in Colorado, Goodman insisted that a team of five experienced and customer-obsessed managers go to Colorado to establish the CC cultural norm of putting the customer first.

- CC involved all employees, right down to the lowest level, in strategy sessions that communicated the company's commitment to its customers and mapped out the economic benefits of its customer obsession (the lifetime value versus cost of acquisition and the critical importance of retaining—and spoiling—all of CC's existing customers).

In 2016, Goodman sold CC. It was a $400 million success story and Goodman attributes much of this success to what she calls her company's "cultural anchor," which she described as "always asking ourselves how much are we helping our customer?"

ThinkCERCA's cofounder and COO Abby Ross tells a different story about her startup's bumpy road to success as a customer-obsessed startup in Chicago. ThinkCERCA (TC) markets CERCA, a research-based framework that helps students engage in critical thinking. (C stands for claim; E stands for evidence; R is for reasoning; C for counterargument; and A for audience.) TC started off focused on its technology and its breakthrough product, but after a near death experience in 2015 (the State of Illinois had stopped paying its bills), TC doubled down on overdelivering results to their customers. In TC's case, this was a particular challenge because it had multiple customers: the student, the student's teacher, and the school district that funded much of TC's CERCA sales. As Ross explains, "We decided to be student- and teacher-centered.

As a social enterprise, we are mission driven; and our mission is helping the student learn." TC found that it had initially recruited too many big-company types who were overly process oriented and not totally aligned with TC's passion for student achievement. The company realized that the best way to make sure that its employees walked around in its customers' shoes was to hire people who really understood the personal challenges and dynamics of the classroom experience involved in teaching in public schools. Over one-third of TC's staff now comprises former teachers. TC's customer-obsessed culture comes naturally to them.

Like CC's Goodman, Diane Hessan built her company's culture on the foundation of doing anything and everything for customers. Communispace was in the listening-to-customers business, so its customer-obsessed culture was perfectly aligned with this mission. Hessan explains: "We ended up with seven values, and being customer focused was number one. We called it 'client dedication.' One reason was that our subscription business model forced us to put our clients first. We lived or died on customer retention, and we didn't want to assume we could do this with our software alone."

At Communispace, employees were expected to respond immediately to calls, emails, and messages from clients, even if these calls came after work hours or on Saturdays or Sundays—and they often did. Competitors used to tell Hessan that they didn't even want to call on Communispace customers because it was a waste of time to try to tempt them to change suppliers. Over the years, as the company grew, its hard earned reputation for being wildly customer centric allowed Communispace to premium price its online communities and grow dramatically from 2002 until it was sold to Omnicom in 2010. Today, now called C Space, with offices in Boston, New York, San Francisco, London, and Shanghai, the customer-obsessed cultural norm is being tested and stretched. But, Charles Trevail, the current CEO, works hard to reinforce and leverage the company's commitment to put customers first. C Space calls itself the "customer agency" and its culture still matches its mission.

Other than walking around in the customer's shoes, what other qualities characterize a customer obsessed–startup culture? Here are six other cultural imperatives for this archetype:

1. Put the customer at the core of the startup's mission statement. Many startups say that they want to change the way something works or revolutionize this or that or even save the world. But unless people can *see, feel,* and *believe* that the company's mission is to make the lives of its customers better, the focus on customers is likely to be fuzzy.

2. Allocate resources to support an obsession with customers. Beef up the customer-service function. Don't put those folks in the basement, make them heroes. Spend money on them. Provide as much technology and support services as possible to customer-facing employees. Expand budgets so that more people can visit customers and engage with them.

3. Measure customer-centric behavior and reward employees based on their customer-focused actions (or lack of them).

4. Talk about customers as real people. Firmly establish pictures of different customer groups in conversations at all levels of the company. Create a sense of *intimacy* with customers. When a startup is small and there are fewer customers—especially in B2B dotcoms—this is easy. Customer-obsessed cultures find ways of keeping this intimacy alive.

5. Keep the big shots in front of customers. Don't delegate face-to-face customer contacts to the sales force or client services or others. If the culture is going to stay customer obsessed, the CEO and all the members of the startup's top team must demonstrate the importance of this obsession by walking the talk themselves.

6. Put in place systems to ensure that you are listening to customers early on. Bring your customers into product decisions, create customer advisory boards, leverage social media to better understand customers' lives, and so on.

Customer-obsessed cultures require a strong emphasis on Passion and an almost equally strong sense of Collaboration. The company must overdeliver on the promises it makes to customers; this usually requires extraordinary effort, whether it means sleeping under the desk at night or responding to customer requests on the weekends. And it often requires the marshaling of resources across organizational boundaries. As the startup grows and new and different customers are acquired, the Learning dimension becomes more important. Last, for the company to be truly responsive to demanding customers, the employees who deal with such customers every day must be empowered to quickly and comprehensively deliver whatever it takes to delight them. Thus, a strong sense of Ownership will need to be part of a customer-obsessed culture.

Customer-obsessed cultures are not perfect places to work, and they certainly aren't for every startup. In many dotcoms the technology or product offer is so obviously superior that other cultural themes will be more important drivers of growth and success. Customers don't have to be spoiled to be loyal. For example, Wayfair, brilliantly led by Niraj Shah, counted more on its software and ever-broader product line to fuel its dramatic growth. Of course, culture mattered a lot at Wayfair, and its culture did focus on good customer service; but Shah and his top team put more stress on the cultural values of speed, agility, and, as Shah says, "getting shit done." Communispace's Hessan admits, "The personal sacrifices needed to live in a customer-obsessed company are not for everyone. We lost a few employees who simply said, 'I want my nights and weekends to myself,' and we accept that."

The biggest challenge for customer-obsessed companies is how to scale the business profitably. In fact, venture capitalists often cringe at the thought that a technology company will make a major investment in a customer-success function for fear that margins will drop and profitable growth will suffer. But startups like CC, Takt, and ClearSky Data have figured out that there are ways to embed customer dialogue and responsive problem resolution right into software, and ways to price and codify customer service so that it can be profitable.

A final note of caution: Customer-obsessed cultures can be expensive. Not every startup can afford to give six months of free service to customers who suffered in a hurricane as CC did. Not every company can spend the money that C Space spends to train and develop all of its customer-facing staff in the skills needed to become their customers' trusted advisors. And not all companies can throw as many in-store staffing resources as Apple did when it launched its retail Apple Store concept.

Archetype 1 Culture Quiz

How Do You Know that
Your Startup Has a Customer-Obsessed Culture?

[1 = nope/never; 5 = maybe/sometimes; 10 = yes/always]

1. Are the big shots in the company frequently and eagerly interacting with customers?

2. Are the client- or customer-service people treated like kings and queens?

3. Is the first and most significant aspect of the company's mission or vision all about making a difference in the lives of your customers?

4. Do most employees know who your biggest customers are and do they know these customers' names?

5. Is customer feedback encouraged, welcomed, and considered a critical part of your company's product development efforts?

6. Are customer satisfaction, customer-retention and/or customer-complaint metrics considered as important as revenue and profit numbers?

7. Are employees who go the extra mile to fix a customer's problem or to respond to a customer's request—no matter how this may upset or disrupt established budgets or procedures—celebrated and rewarded?

8. Do the startup's investors and board of directors believe that an obsession with overdelivering value to customers is the right growth strategy?

9. Do you go to the company's website and read about customer stories more than about the company's products?

10. Do you see the customer in the company's physical space in the form of photos, logos, awards, case studies and more?

Archetype 2: The Take-Care-of-You Culture

Nobody expects startups to be easy, relaxing, vacationlike places to work. Entrepreneurs are driven to succeed and they want to be surrounded by similarly driven people. But a surprising number of successful startups have cultures that emphasize the Caring dimension. A take-care-of-you culture is not a paternalistic culture; it has a more home-away-from-home ethos. Some entrepreneurs have discovered that to hire and retain talented engineers, salespeople and bean counters, they have to create an environment that literally substitutes for the personal life that is often left behind in other organizations. Plentiful food, comfortable places to work, lots of reward and recognition, frequent check-in meetings with employees and their managers, and regular, fun-filled events are some of the perks. This works well with younger employees. They are expected—and love) to work 12 or 15 hours a day in an environment that values them as humans, cares about their careers, and takes care of their needs. They like being fed, entertained, hugged, and supported emotionally. In addition to clypd, described above, two other startups closely resemble this archetype: Tribe Dynamics and ezCater.

Tribe Dynamics is an online marketing company founded in 2012 by Jon Namnath and Conor Begley. When you go to its website, you can see the company's four values listed in order:

- Caring

- Learning

- Simple, and

- SWAS (software with amazing service)

Caring is described as follows: "Designed and built with love. Good business is about great relationships. This extends through our code and everything we do. We care about our people. We care about our customers. We care about the world."

This cultural emphasis has proved a successful magnet for over two-dozen talented engineers. Unlike many Bay Area startups, Begley insists that all of his employees work in the Tribe Dynamics office. "This is the best way to leverage our culture. It makes it easier to collaborate and more like a family."

Tribe Dynamics' culture is reinforced by the way Begley and his top team run the place—some examples of the practices that signal to employees that the company cares are:

- It invests in quarterly retreats, where relationships are strengthened.

- New employees have peer buddies to make sure they become quickly connected to the company and its values.

- Slack workflow software is used constantly to keep personal and business conversations going all the time.

- Wednesdays are game days and the game activities often go into the evenings.

- Every Friday is an all-hands lunch and an open-forum town hall meeting to encourage sharing and relationship building.

ezCater is an online business catering startup that now operates in over 22,000 cities all over the US. It has what it calls a "culture recipe." The phrase "taking care of you" is not explicitly mentioned as one of the nine recipe ingredients, but over the years Stefania Mallett, ezCater's CEO, has consistently sent signals to her entire organization that the company's culture is highly supportive. "We are a software-enabled service company, which means that our success formula is all about humans. Software gets written by humans, and service is delivered either by clever software or directly by humans. I spend 45 to 60 minutes with every batch of new employees in which I emphasize 'Without you, we are nothing.' At the end of this introduction, the new employees often break into warm applause." Mallett and her top team communicate ezCater's commitment to taking care of its employees in lots of other ways:

- Employees who act in accordance with the nine culture-recipe ingredients are given cupcakes and are widely recognized.

- When Mallett discovered that someone kept locking the snack cabinet, she went to the people who locked the cabinet and asked them for their reasoning. She learned that they carried old habits from previous cultures. After discussion, it was agreed to unlock the cabinet and see what happened. "Good families don't lock cabinet doors so people can't get to the goodies."

- Interestingly, ezCater is a very data and measurements-driven company and this helps reinforce the personally supportive culture. As Mallett explains, "Numbers don't lie. They keep us focused. We simply don't have arguments about which is the 'right way' to go. It makes our company a psychologically safer place."

- When ezCater had to let an otherwise high performer go because he failed to take care of his people and treated them poorly, Mallett learned that these employees hadn't come forward earlier to blow the whistle on the offending manager because, as they said, "We didn't want to harm the company in any way because it has been so good to us."

- At ezCater, employees don't use the term "work-life balance." They refer to "life-work balance." This may sound small to an outsider, but it is a big difference to the company's employees.

A startling fact emerged in a focus-group meeting with ezCater employees from all parts and levels of the company. When shown the seven culture dimensions described in Chapter 2, these employees were asked two questions: (1) which dimension of culture did they feel was most important in driving their personal performance, and (2) which dimension did they feel was most important in contributing to their personal satisfaction. Not surprisingly, 83 percent said that the Caring dimension was the top contributor to personal satisfaction. But an equal number (83 percent of the members who were in the focus group) said that a culture dominated by Caring was the primary performance motivator.

The implication of all of this for startup entrepreneurs is that if you create a strong take-care-of-you culture, many young and talented people will respond and work like hell to make the company a success. In startup cultures like those at clypd, Tribe Dynamics and ezCater, employees said over and over again: "I work hard, but it is my choice to do so." The mutual respect and support found in a great Caring culture make it much easier to foster high levels of both Collaboration and Transparency. After all, people want to work closely with those they trust and leaders who openly share lots of information.

The take-care-of-you companies tend to have high rates of

employee retention and will often talk about their boomerangs—employees who leave, often for more money, who then return, because it just isn't the same in the new place. These companies also often subscribe to the "employees first" policy, believing that if you take care of your employees, they will, in turn, take care of customers—and that translates into taking care of the company.

A take-care-of-you culture has more than a few drawbacks. As the ezCater whistleblower story illustrates, it can lead people to avoid conflict. It may also lead some employees to think that performance standards are lowered, or that being nice is valued more than being productive. But the biggest issue with this startup-culture archetype is that it is hard to scale. Startups with one office can be a home away from home; larger companies with multiple offices, more employees, and less intimate leadership will find it hard to replicate this kind of culture. ezCater now has over 170 employees, and its culture continues to be a source of competitive advantage. It was Mallett who said, "Culture eats strategy for breakfast." But she works very hard to deal with this scaling issue. Without intentional efforts to reinforce (and even codify) the take-care-of-you employee experience as a startup grows, you often hear people whispering, "It's just not as great a place as it used to be."

It's important to distinguish between companies that truly care about their employees and those that fake it.

There are startups that feed their employees great breakfasts starting at 7:00am because they want their people to start the day early. As one cynical Silicon Valley engineer remarked: "By 9:00 all that's left are the bagels." The vast majority of startup employees in the research sample were confident that they could tell the difference.

Archetype 2 Culture Quiz

How Do You Know that
Your Startup Has a Take-Care-of-You Culture?

[1 = nope/never; 5 = maybe/sometimes; 10 = yes/always]

1. Does the company offer "all the comforts of home" like free breakfasts, lunches, and even dinner?

2. Are all new job candidates screened thoroughly for personalities that can fit into a culture that places a premium on caring?

3. Does the startup's digital and physical presence feature lots of pictures of company employees "hanging out" and in social situations?

4. Do the founders and leaders keep talking about the importance of mutual respect, caring, "winning as a team," and other relationship-oriented themes?

5. Is the company's Glass Door rating 4.8 or better?

6. Is the vast majority of the startup's leaders part of the original management team?

7. Do the big shots write personal happy birthday or anniversary notes (and sometimes give gifts) to employees?

8. Does the company invest in events largely focused on employees getting to know each other better?

9. Does the company's benefits plan include lots of care-for-you perks like stress management training, unlimited vacations, career counseling, and medical services that come to the office?

10. Do you see other comforts of home in the company's offices, such as beanbag chairs, a "mother's room" or day care facilities? Are dogs roaming the hallways and featured on the company's website?

Archetype 3: The Performance-Driven Culture

Back in 1965, a series of experiments were conducted at the Harvard Business School in which researchers successfully created what they called a "high achieving" startup culture. In this laboratory culture, employees of the startup experienced

- very high performance standards;

- lots of performance feedback—to individuals and to teams;

- high levels of individual responsibility;

- an emphasis on innovation, and

- an intense focus on out-performing the competition.

The lead researcher on these experiments, George Litwin, concluded that just as some people are motivated by a need to win and outperform a self-imposed standard of excellence, the same goes for entire organizations, particularly those that are aggressively competing for market share, growth or profitability. (These experiments are described more fully in Appendix A.)

Fast-forward to the 21st century, and such performance-driven cultures can be found all over the startup world. They are successful because they encourage—some would say demand—extraordinary effort. Armed with 21st-century technology, they employ all sorts of measures to track the results of that effort. In performance-driven startup cultures, the founders work 24/7 and so does everyone else. People take pride in sleeping under their desks when necessary. Everyone in the company knows the metrics, which often become part of the culture's language. Listen to this: "Our CAC is down from $40.25 to $38.41 this month. Even better, our RPE is now up to $582,341." (CAC is customer acquisition cost and RPE is revenue per employee.)

Successful performance-driven cultures are easy to spot. They are agile, open, and constantly measuring themselves against all sorts of benchmarks and standards. At least three startups in the research sample come to mind: Shoebuy (a ecommerce company), Wayfair (another ecommerce company), and Halo Neuroscience (medical technology startup).

Scott Savitz founded Shoebuy in 1999, and helped grow the company to over $200 million in revenues in 2011, before its sale to Barry Diller's IAC. Savitz was (and still is) a metrics freak. At Shoebuy, he used "midnight reports" to continuously measure the performance of individuals and functions. Remarkably, he let his people choose the metrics that they would be measured on. But he and his top team always paid close attention to the numbers. And so did everyone else at Shoebuy. As Savitz says: "I wanted every employee to see if they were winning or losing." According to Savitz, industry knowledge and experience counted for far less than a person's motivation. "A-team players were the key to our culture and the key to our success. I hired 'athletes'—people who were really competitive and worked really hard." At Shoebuy, this proved to be a winning formula.

The success formula at Wayfair, according to cofounder Niraj Shah, is very simple: "Use our online platform to sell as much stuff for the home to as many people as possible." From its beginning in 2002, Steve Conine (the other cofounder) and Shah have built a $3.5 billion business that offers 7 million products from over 7,000 suppliers and operates throughout North America and Europe. From the beginning, Wayfair hired its employees right out of school. Shah's leadership team looked for smart graduates who had "lots of energy . . . and didn't mind working their asses off. We wanted high achievers, and we got them." Today, with over 5,600 employees, Shah sees one of his most important jobs at Wayfair as minimizing processes that slow things down. "It's harder now," Shah admits, "but as a young startup, Steve and I knew that speed and agility were the only way we were going to win. Wayfair's culture was based on that premise."

Other aspects of Wayfair's early performance-driven culture

enhanced and complemented the high expectations for getting shit done. And Shah believes they still serve the company well in 2017:

- Wayfair is data-driven. This means that at all levels of the organization, people know what success is. The most important kind of performance feedback is in the numbers.

- Performance goals and expectations are clear and widely communicated.

- Wayfair tolerates turnover. Shah admits that some people find the company's emphasis on results and performance unsettling. He's okay with that, and Wayfair's rapid growth seems to make employee loyalty a less important part of its success formula.

- Wayfair leaders have committed themselves to a culture of meritocracy. As Shah declares: "We place a greater value on meritocracy than we do on loyalty."

The Wayfair performance-driven culture includes an emphasis on empowerment and letting people achieve with a minimum of top-down management. "In the beginning, we didn't hire many expensive big shots. We were largely self-funded and decided to spend our money on 'doers,' not executives. We gave our young employees plenty of freedom."

Even though Wayfair's size disqualifies it from being a startup in 2017, Shah believes that the company still has a powerful performance-driven culture. "You stay with what works. As long as the founders stay put and continue to lead the way they did in the beginning, the startup culture will stick. It may morph a bit, but the basic principles and values will be there."

Halo Neuroscience (HN) has a different kind of performance-driven culture. Daniel Chao and Brett Wingeier cofounded the company in 2014 and self-funded it until they had a working prototype of the brain-stimulating technology that they now manufacture and sell as HaloSport. Like Wayfair, HN decided to hire young, achievement-oriented graduates from schools like Stanford, Harvard and Princeton. Chao explains: "We went after smart, motivated grads. They didn't need any particular expertise . . . only drive. Bret and I knew how to do their jobs, so these earliest hires were easy to train. Once we geared up and raised our first $7 million (in 2015), we started hiring more engineers. And in 2016, we pivoted again and hired really smart, young, design and marketing types. All 20 of our employees have different skills; but they all want to win!"

Chao uses a performance-driven metaphor to illustrate the HN culture: "I liken a startup to a canoe or scull or rowboat. We are paddling upstream. Unless you paddle harder, we'll all go backwards. We paddle like crazy here, and we can feel what progress is like. We all have a great sense of accomplishment and achievement." Each Monday, every employee sets his or her goals for the week. Managers review these goals, and on Friday, they are used to measure personal and team progress. Chao hands out a paddle (that contains every HN employee's signature on it) to the top performers. If insufficient progress has been made, the usual Friday happy hour is cancelled. Not surprisingly, this rarely happens.

Like all performance-driven startup cultures, HN prides itself on having a high-feedback work environment. As Chao summarizes, "Feedback is a gift, especially performance feedback. We want our people to get in the habit of getting it and giving it."

Performance-driven startup cultures require a distinctive combination of the seven cultural imperatives described at the beginning of this chapter. Passion—a passion for winning—is critical. So is Ownership—it is the sense of being personally accountable for delivering results that motivates high achievers. And most performance-driven cultures feature a certain amount of Messiness, Collaboration, and Transparency. People are too busy getting shit done to worry about policies or procedures. They need to be able to grab resources from other parts of the organization to get the work done quickly and efficiently. And they need to always know how they and the company are doing,

What are the pitfalls of a performance-driven culture? The most obvious one is burnout. Being constantly measured, evaluated and under pressure isn't everyone's cup of tea. Startups characterized by a constant pressure to perform—without providing people with emotional and social support—will find it hard to attract and retain top talent. And, without great talent, they will not be able to scale. Wayfair seems to have the right balance of cultural dimensions, but if Shah and Conine should leave, its performance-driven culture may prove to be unsustainable. These two founders have a unique leadership style and their personal priorities and values form a large part of Wayfair's culture. Another pitfall is the unintended message that performance-driven cultures can send to customers. If customers or clients feel that they are "being sold" by an overly aggressive and desperate account rep, it will backfire. When pressed, Shah admitted that, because of the non-personal online relationships established by the company's business model, Wayfair's customers didn't really "feel" the company's performance emphasis. Upselling was less a function of a sales person "pushing" for another order, than it was the technology platform "guiding" customers to new products or offers.

Finally, some performance-driven startups find themselves chasing the wrong set of performance metrics. For example, Smart Lunches, a startup that is trying to scale its online ordering and delivery service for nutritious school lunches, originally focused—and rewarded its performance-driven business developers—on acquiring new accounts in the markets it served. The problem was that signing up small schools (which drove up the number of new accounts) wreaked havoc with the bottom line. After several years of unprofitable growth, the company switched its focus to selling more lunches to existing accounts. This helped streamline their deliveries and dramatically improved their profitability.

Archetype 3 Culture Quiz

How Do You Know that
Your Startup Has a Performance-Driven Culture?

[1 = nope/never; 5 = maybe/sometimes; 10 = yes/always]

1. Does everyone in the company have explicit performance goals and targets?

2. Do the leaders of the startup constantly talk about winning, outcompeting, or beating out other companies for new business?

3. Does everyone—especially the top people—keep score? Do there seem to be performance metrics for everything?

4. Are the highest performers the ones who are rewarded and promoted?

5. Are there usually competitive activities (with winners and losers) at company off-sites or gatherings?

6. Do people comment about how demanding the place is? Or how expectations are so high that it often seems impossible to meet them?

7. Are there charts and graphs on the company's walls and in all of its presentations to staff and the board?

8. Does the recruiting team have a bias for hiring people who were on athletic teams in school?

9. Do the startup's leaders emphasize topics like failing fast, overcoming obstacles, and taking risks?

10. Do employees feel pride in the hours they work and are they open about how they manage their stress?

Archetype 4: The Product-Innovation Culture

While some startups win by obsessing over customers or being a home away from home or simply outdoing competitors, a good many win by constant product innovation. Their success formula is all about building the most dazzling, leading-edge technology products, and then keeping those products on the leading edge of technology. To do that, startup founders must create a culture that will attract and retain the most talented software engineers possible. What motivates these hotshot engineers and data scientists? They want time to explore new variations of the software. They want colleagues who are as smart or smarter than they are. They want plenty of freedom to test and try out their ideas. They often have high levels of achievement motivation (once again, review Appendix A for the Harvard Business School research study of achievement motivation). They want to keep learning, and to build their resumes with expertise in the newest and greatest technology products. They like the feeling that the product is never done, never perfected, and that their job is all about discovering the next cool platform or application. For these folks, if they're not learning and inventing, they're bored and looking for their next job—in a company with a better culture of product innovation.

Disruptor Beam is a good example of a successful product innovation culture. Founded in 2010 by Jon Radoff, Disruptor Beam is a developer and publisher of branded mobile and web games like Star Trek Timelines and Game of Thrones Ascent. One of the reasons Radoff started the company (it is his third) was to create the best possible environment for game developers. As he describes it, "The game industry really sucks. It's dominated by publishers who see developers as totally replaceable drones on a death march to some predetermined publishing date. I want to build a long-term growth company that will hire and *keep* the best talent in the industry." Radoff feels that his company's culture is a powerful strategic weapon. "I want this to be my last startup, so I am paying close attention to our culture. I think it may be possible for some dotcoms to have a lousy culture and succeed for a while. But, if you get the right kind of culture, it will multiply all aspects of performance—revenues, profits, innovation, and customer loyalty."

Disruptor Beam's website describes what the kind of new hires it wants: "[W]e're looking for humble but ambitious, razor-sharp professionals who can teach us a thing or two. We promise to return the favor. These individuals will become part of entrepreneurial teams who prefer action (kicking ass) over process and bureaucracy (taking names). We embrace those who see things differently, who aren't afraid to experiment, and who have a healthy disregard for the rules." When you insist on hiring people who want to learn and experiment, you are building a startup with a product innovation culture.

Like Disruptor Beam, ClearSky Data (CSD) is another successful engineering-driven startup in Boston that has a product innovation culture. Founded in 2014 by Ellen Rubin and Lazarus Vekiarides, CSD builds and deploys breakthrough data-storage technology solutions for enterprise-size corporations. CSD is Rubin's third startup: "We have hardcore developer types who are incredibly smart problem solvers. They are data-driven. They want to be able to ask lots of questions and understand the why of decisions. And they want to be challenged—they *have* to be challenged or they won't stay." Rubin points to a number of things that she feels are important determinants of CSD's product innovation culture:

- "From the very start, Laz and I were on the same page about the culture that we wanted to have. That was critically important to both of us."

- An open floor plan that includes gathering areas—open spaces where small groups of people can meet and brainstorm. Passersby are encouraged to listen in, thus expanding the potential source of new product ideas.

- Very few closed off conference rooms.

- An emphasis on humor. "Humor often expands the agenda in our conversations," Rubin says. "It's safe to be a bit edgy, hopefully in a way that is constructive."

- Adhering to the O'Hare Airport–rule when hiring people. ("How would we feel getting stuck at O'Hare for four hours with this person?")

Gfycat is a Silicon Valley startup that develops and operates a web-based platform that allows customers to share videos. The company describes its technology as "GIFs done right." (GIF is an acronym for graphic interchange format, a moving web image.) GIFs have been around since the 1980s, but Richard Rabbat, Dan McEleney and Jeff Harris founded Gfycat in 2015. They worked part time for four years before that time and now employ 15 people, mostly engineers. "We have to convince a bunch of really smart people to join us," Rabbat explains. "And in order to do that, you have to have the right kind of work environment. Hell, we are competing for talent against Google."

What is the right kind of work environment for Gfycat? In Rabbat's own words, it is open, friendly, innovative and supportive. "All I know is that we have to value everyone's ideas. We can't shut people down. One of these days, we will have to document our cultural priorities and principles, but we haven't done that yet."

Gfycat's success, of course, is not just a function of its culture. It's in a hot market. Demand for their hosting platform is exploding. In mid–2017, the website was the 60th most popular site in the US . . . and growing more popular every month. But, without the emphasis and attention paid to "letting our engineers innovate," Rabbat says, he knows his company would not be where it is.

At Disruptor Beam, ClearSky Data, and Gfycat, out-of-the-box thinking, new ideas, and invention are the name of the game. Product innovation–driven startup Rippleshot's Tran (who speaks about Passion in Chapter 2's seven dimensions section) sums it up: "It's really hard to recruit and retain top-notch data scientists and engineers; as a startup, you just don't have the money to pay a lot. So having a safe, collaborative place, open to any kind of crazy new product idea where smart people can talk about anything—that's the draw."

Product innovation cultures put a big emphasis on the Learning dimension, as you may expect. People are encouraged to try something new, and if it doesn't work, to try something else. They're expected to learn by doing and to continuously improve both the product and their own skills. And, they value the chance to work alongside others who can help them learn new ways to code or new architectures or new ways to think about data. Along with Learning, product innovation cultures also tend to have high levels of both Collaboration and Messiness. As both Tran and Rubin point out, Collaboration is essential because new product ideas don't happen in a vacuum; sharing and discussion are an important part of innovation. Plus, getting a new product idea developed quickly requires moving the right resources around from wherever they are in the organization to create a team that can work together to get the job done. Product innovation–driven startups are typically very messy. Lots of reinvention and continuous development don't require explicit procedures. The fact that the rulebook hasn't been written yet is no barrier to a successful startup with a product innovation culture.

A potential pitfall for product innovation–driven startups is becoming so enamored with new technological bells and whistles that they ignore customers' needs. A creative technology tweak may be exciting to a software developer, but is it actually something the customer *wants*? Staying plugged in to customers and what they need helps keep innovation junkies grounded in the real world of customer-centric growth.

Scaling a startup with a product innovation culture is challenging. Continued success depends on attracting and retaining a constant stream of high-level engineering talent. Many startups that rely on technology innovation end up putting processes and procedures in place that tend to discourage the free-wheeling behaviors that led to their initial success. As Google, LinkedIn, and Apple prove, it can be done. But Rippleshot's Tran speaks for many entrepreneurs who are betting on a product innovation culture: "Those early days can be superheady—R&D is king, with lots of frenzy, creativity, and innovation. For the business to grow, though, you must realize that people have to focus more on executing what has already been developed. They have to stop constantly pushing their latest and greatest ideas. You have to nail down a few processes and that will be tough for some engineers to accept."

Archetype 4 Culture Quiz

How Do You Know
that Your Startup Has an Innovation Culture?

[1 = nope/never; 5 = maybe/sometimes; 10 = yes/always]

1. Are other startups and high-tech companies constantly recruiting your best engineers?

2. Are experiments that don't work and failed approaches accepted and even applauded?

3. Does the company hold frequent meetings to showcase new product ideas and new approaches?

4. Do you have development days or hackathons where people are expected to work on one of their own product ideas?

5. Do employees talk about how proud they are to work with the smartest people on the planet?

6. Do you tend to hire creative types even if they don't fit a particular job category?

7. Are the engineers kings? Are they the ones with the status in the company?

8. Is there a constant stream of new features and new releases in the company's products?

9. Does leadership talk more about the product than the business results?

10. Are there constant messages to employees asking for help hiring the best engineers in the country?

Archetype 5: The Frat Culture

If the previous four archetypes describe a possible cultural success formula for startups, this archetype doesn't. The frat-culture (fraternity-like) phenomenon has received a boatload of press recently, all of it highlighting the fact that these kinds of cultures only work for a short period of time. Founders who create frat cultures are always men, and they want to work with people who not only share their excitement about the new venture, but who look like them, talk like them, laugh at the same jokes, drink the same booze, and enjoy the same extracurricular activities. Many times, startups with frat cultures are filled with guys who went to the same school, or at least shared a more or less common fraternity house experience in school. They are used to working hard and playing hard.

And it works, but only for a while. The frat culture's male comradeship is often coupled with employees with high levels of achievement motivation, a willingness to take risks and admit mistakes, and an interpersonal candor that keeps the ideas flowing and the energy high. Stuff gets done. As long as the startup has a winning product, market acceptance, and enough funding, the culture isn't a big issue to these founders. As Michael Patak, cofounder of TopStepTrader, remembers: "When I started, I didn't really think about our culture. It was just us guys. I knew how to trade commodities and make a lot of money, and we had a system for teaching what I knew to others. We were self-funded, so I didn't have to pay much attention to what others might think about our culture."

Catalant Technologies also began its success trajectory as a frat culture. Rob Biederman, its founder, graduated from HBS in 2013 and started Catalant as a student. By the time he graduated in 2014, he had 20 employees—mostly friends of his. One Catalant observer commented: "If you saw their loft office on Broomfield Street, you'd say it looked like a frat house...files and food and work all over the place and a bunch of guys having a blast making sales calls on everyone they could in the Cambridge and Boston area."

The biggest problem with the frat-culture archetype is that it loses its efficacy when the startup scales. The culture turns from an asset to a liability. If the founders want to build a larger, successful business, the culture is either going to have to morph into a more sustainable work environment, or it's going to implode. Frat cultures have two major drawbacks.

The first major drawback is unethical practices, which in the insular, overly macho, and aggressive value system of most frat cultures lead to moral lapses, bad behavior, and rule breaking. Founders and their buddies feel that they can do no wrong. Early successes reinforce this feeling. A 2015 article in *The Journal of Business Ethics* pointed out that two factors make it tempting for frat cultures to encourage the fudging of ethical questions: the relative lack of oversight at startups and the high likelihood of failure. Think of Martin Shkreli, founder of Turing Pharmaceuticals. He's in jail. Or Uber's Travis Kalanick or Parker Conrad, the founder and ousted CEO of human resources software firm Zenefits. These are not startup-culture heroes.

The second major drawback is lack of diversity. There simply aren't enough fraternity brothers to build a big company. The eat-drink-play similarity found in frat cultures ultimately makes it impossible to recruit and retain enough talent. Women aren't attracted to frat cultures, nor are minorities, foreign-born engineers, or older workers. It's a matter of basic supply and demand, and competitors with healthier startup cultures will simply win over frat cultures.

The classic example of a successful frat culture that ultimately stumbled is Uber. It had everything going for it: a revolutionary service with widespread market acceptance, a unique business model that treated drivers as contractors rather than actual employees, access to a seemingly unlimited amount of private capital, and a growth strategy that knew no bounds. But, it also had Travis Kalanick, who built Uber's culture in his own image and hired people who were similarly driven.

Under Kalanick's leadership, Uber developed a tool to evade regulators, had dozens of employees allege sexual harassment or discrimination, and was accused of stealing intellectual property from a rival. In the beginning, people called these practices "innovations," but after a while it was obvious that Uber's rule breaking was really cheating.

Kalanick was pushed out as Uber CEO in the spring of 2017, along with 20 other of his buddies. The papers are full of stories about what went wrong. By the time this book is published, we'll probably all know a lot more about it, but there is no question that the profound truth about Uber—other than startup cultures matter a lot—is that leadership drives culture. And that is especially true for frat cultures.

My bet is that Uber will not go under, but it will no longer enjoy the market dominance it once had. So, eight years after its founding, can Uber's culture be changed? Will replacing Kalanick with new Uber CEO Dara Khosrowshahi do the trick? He recently had Uber employees vote on new cultural guidelines that included such themes as "we celebrate differences," "we act as owners," "we value ideas over hierarchy," and "we are customer obsessed."[1] We will see if these new guidelines (which replaced themes like "always be hustling," "let builders build," and "meritocracy and toe-stepping") serve to motivate a change in the Uber culture.[2]

Farhad Manjoo, a technology writer for *The New York Times*, points to the lack of public scrutiny as one of the barriers to startup culture reform. Regarding Uber, he writes, "Staying private created a hothouse that reinforced its worst side, and allowed it to delay building a sustainable culture with a focus on long-term interests.[3]

Other startups that have experienced the limits of a frat culture include Upload, Social Finance, and Magic Leap. These companies imploded due to sexual harassment accusations leveled against various leaders in these firms. The pernicious culture of sexism within these companies is sometimes mirrored in the VC firms that invest in them. For example, 500 Startups, Binary Capital, and Kleiner Perkins have all been accused of having frat cultures. According to Joan Williams, a professor at Hastings College of Law: "When work becomes a masculinity contest, whether it's measuring the hours you're working or the pay you're making, then often hitting on the women in the office is just another metric of your success there." [4]

Unlike these companies, Catalant Technologies has outgrown its initial frat culture and enjoyed three years of steady growth without drama or complaints. The keys to Catalant's success are easy to identify. First, Catalant CEO Rob Biederman is no Travis Kalanick. Biederman is an all-around entrepreneurial leader who realized shortly after his company hired its 40th employee that the Catalant culture needed attention. He took the time to lead an all-hands meeting to define the company's cultural principles, and made sure that these included an emphasis on diversity and inclusion. In other words, Catalant morphed its male-dominated culture to one that embraces women, minorities, and people who were different from Biederman and his early hires.

Employees in frat cultures experience Messiness and Collaboration. They can also sense a fair amount of Learning, Transparency and Caring, although these cultural dimensions tend to have their own variation in the male-dominated frat culture world. Learning requires an especially thick skin. Transparency sometimes requires employees to understand the code words and sports analogies that are used so often; and Caring means that your home away from home could resemble a sports bar. With growth, Messiness turns into sloppiness. And Learning can turn into a "get out of my way—I have the answer" attitude. Like what happened to Uber, Social Finance, Upload, and Magic Leap, the culture takes on a certain amount of insularity and arrogance. Although the intent is quality and innovation, the result is often a macho culture that doesn't welcome outsiders or question its own mores or norms.

Archetype 5 Culture Quiz

How Do You Know that Your Startup Has a Frat Culture?

[1 = nope/never; 5 = maybe/sometimes; 10 = yes/always]

1. Are over 80 percent of your employees men?
2. Do you find it much harder to recruit women to fill your job openings than to recruit men?

3. Is the boundary between work and play fuzzy, and is there sometimes is a party atmosphere in the office?

4. Are there stories with pictures of young female employees on social media sites about what it's like to work at your startup?

5. Are female employees (other than maintenance staff) expected to do the cleaning up around the office?

6. If employees feel uncomfortable about their experiences in the company, have you ignored the need for an outside ombudsman for these employees to talk to?

7. If employees have complaints about how they are treated, are they expected to just suck it up?

8. Is it common for the men in the office to date or have intimate relationships with the women in the company?

9. Are most of the jokes and stories told in the office sexually oriented in some way?

10. Do male employees make a lot of comments on the women's looks and dress?

Would-be entrepreneurs should think hard about the attributes, consequences and dynamics of these five cultural archetypes. The culture quizzes will help you size up the kind of culture that may currently exist in your company, but the most successful founders think about the culture they want before they start to build their business. Unfortunately, startup cultures don't just materialize from the founders' minds. They come from a complex series of factors that must be understood to be constructively managed.

CHAPTER 4

Where Startup Cultures Come From

T HE CULTURE OF an organization—what people experience when they join and work in a company—comes from three basic sources: (1) the people in the organization, (2) the physical surroundings and rules that govern people's behavior, and (3) the external factors the organization faces. For entrepreneurs and leaders of startups, it's really important to understand how these three culture determinants impact people's experiences, feelings, and personal motivation.

People

By far the most influential source of a startup's culture is the founder and/or cofounders. They are the people who set the tone, have the most powerful impact on what others experience, and control most of the input into the roots of a startup's culture. It is critically important for the founders to share a common sense of purpose, complementary values, and a commitment to working together. Mixed messages about cultural norms and conflicting founder statements and behaviors will weaken—and eventually dissipate—a startup's culture. Silicon Valley VC Peter Thiel emphasizes this point: "Technical abilities and complementary skill sets matter, but how well the founders know each other and how well they work together matter just as much."[1] VC Ron Croen agrees: "The founders' values define a startup's culture. Cofounders need not have exactly the same leadership styles, but their values must be the same and, if the startup is going to be successful, they sure as hell must send a consistent message about what's important."

One of the clearest signals of the founders' values and cultural priorities is who's recruited to round out the startup's leadership team. Entrepreneurs who have founded multiple startups drive home the point that the earliest hires are critical to defining the company's culture. T.J. Mahony, founder of FlipKey and now a VC, believes, "Culture starts at the top. The first four people you hire will make all of the difference. That's why so many successful startup CEOs insist on interviewing every single person they are trying to recruit." Shoebuy's Savitz reiterates this point: "For the first year, I made it a point to interview every candidate. That's how important our early hires were to me."

First-time founders often find themselves in a bind when they hire technical wizards and disregard a person's interpersonal and relationship skills. Here, three observations and warnings from first-time startup CEOs:

- Halo Neuroscience's Daniel Chao (founder and CEO): "I learned the hard way that one bad leadership hire will have a profound, negative influence on the company's culture."

- Sequoia's Golub (founder and CEO): "My most important decisions are people decisions. We have a Sequoia Fit [list of attributes] that we use to bring on new client-services talent. We really try to dig into people's character, and ask ourselves, 'How will it feel being around this person all of the time?' When we fail to do this, it's expensive. It always comes back to bite us."

- Caaapital's Capurro (founder and CEO): "I'm not losing sleep over how the business is doing. We are doing great. My big worry is whether people 'fit' into our entrepreneurial culture. Technically, a person can be top-notch but everyone has to be on the same page when it comes to our working relationships . . . you know, the soft stuff."

Startup cultures are not solely determined by the founders or the leadership team (although these two sources of culture are the most potent). All the members of a young and relatively small organization contribute to the startup's culture. As FlipKey's Mahony says, "The first 20 people have to feel that their fingerprints are all over the business. That's how you have a culture of ownership." clypd's Summers explains it this way: "You can't always consciously design a startup culture. It's a living organism. Every new hire will invariably change the organism . . . so that's why hiring the right people is so critical."

Is there a point at which startup entrepreneurs can relax when it comes to the people they bring into the organization? Not according to those in the research sample. As Katie Burke, the chief people officer at HubSpot, says, "We pay just as much attention to the people we hire, now that we have over 400 employees, as we did when there were only 40. We've documented our culture and tell candidates what it's like to work here. And we don't worry if some folks are turned off and walk away."

There is a Catch-22 here. In general, people are the most important determinant of the work environment of a startup. What people say, how they treat one another, what they do, and what they don't do all mold the cultural norms and establish the unwritten rules and expectations that define a culture. But people are notoriously complex and unpredictable. They are a diverse bundle of motives, fears, ambitions, neuroses, and personalities. No job interview process is going to be 100 percent effective in identifying the winners and weeding out the losers. Nonetheless, the key to building the right kind of startup culture is to make your people decisions a supercritical priority. Ben Horowitz, author of *The Hard Thing About Hard Things*, sends a loud and clear message to startup founders: "When you start implementing your culture, keep in mind that most of what will be retrospectively referred to as your company's culture will not have been designed into the system, but rather will have evolved over time based on your behavior and the behavior of your early employees."[2]

So how do the leaders of successful startups screen for the people who best fit their culture and who will make the best members of the startup team? There is no magic formula, for every company is different, every hiring manager has his or her favorites and blind spots, and every candidate (especially those who are in demand and have been through dozens of interviews) will react differently. Below is a sampling of screening techniques that have worked for successful startup leaders:

- "I tend to focus on questions around self-awareness. What kind of environments do you thrive in, and which do you find stifling? [I] also ask people what their triggers are. If an executive can't answer what their triggers are, that's a nonstarter. We all have them, and if you're not aware of them that probably means you lack maturity around them. If they're aware of their triggers, I ask them how they manage them." (Rapid7's Thomas)

- "I look for an incredibly high degree of curiosity—people who just relentlessly want to learn new things and put themselves in new situations—and a high degree of empathy. If people are curious and empathetic, they can learn just about anything. One of the best ways to tell whether someone's curious and empathetic is to ask them [what] questions they have. You can see how their minds work and how thoughtful they are." (Matthew Prince, CEO of Cloudflare)

- "I always look for athletes—people who were really competitive—then I would figure out where to put them. If a candidate had a history of winning, and talked about winning, that was much more important to me than a pedigree." (Shoebuy's Savitz)

- "We look for people who have endurance; people who take charge and are in control of their own destiny. In a startup, we want people who bring their whole self to work, so we screen out those who won't share their personal life stories." (Shradha Agarwal, founder of Outcome Health)

- "We interview to weed out the 'assholes.' That means lots of different people screen a candidate. We also are looking for people who are flexible and adaptive. We call them 'rovers' and we try to hire rovers." (CC's Goodman)

- "In the beginning, I looked for talented people that I already knew. When we explained who we were and what the company was all about, these folks had a high level of trust that was critically important. They assumed that we'd be fair. Many said 'yes' before we even talked money." (Shorelight Education's Dretler)

- "Here in San Francisco, we see all types of creative engineering talent. You wouldn't believe what people wear to an interview. So we look for candidates who are presentable. That shows a certain respect for others. We also want people who are excited. One other thing that we do is probe to learn about people's failures. How they talk about past mistakes and failures is a sign of a person's basic honesty . . . and that the kind we want." (Gfycat's Rabbat)

The Startup Institute, a for-profit educational company run by CEO Rich DiTieri that runs a boot camp for individuals who want jobs in startups, has identified six characteristics of successful employees at rapidly growing companies. Its research parallels the research conducted for *Culture.com: How the Best Startups Make It Happen*, and the findings shed light on what startup leaders should be looking for if they want to hire talent that "fits." Here's their list of the most important skills that the leaders of rapidly growing businesses want to see:

- Desire to learn
- Ability to thrive amidst ambiguity
- Passion
- Scrappiness and grit
- Excellence at collaboration, and
- Willingness to put the company before oneself

Not surprisingly, there is an almost perfect match between the seven attributes of winning startup cultures and the characteristics that the leaders of companies trying to grow rapidly want to see. (Appendix D contains the full Startup Institute research report.)

Space, Processes, and Other Rules of the Road

Space

The space that a startup occupies can be a significant contributor to the culture. People spend so much time at work that their surroundings often contribute directly to how they feel about their jobs. Key decisions like whether people have open or closed offices, what visitors see when they enter, what colors and visual elements are in play, and what kinds of common areas exist all are important elements of a startup's space.

The vast majority of startups in the research sample opted for an open-space design, with few, if any, closed-off offices. Workstations, coffee and kitchen facilities, and conference rooms and play areas, were visible and open to all. Wayfair's Shah, some 15 years ago, believed his company's open-office layout always fostered both Transparency and

Collaboration. "Open offices were not all that common back in 2002, but we believed that our choice of an open design would not only be more economical, it would [also] help us be more agile. Our office space to us was part of our culture."

Like Shah, most entrepreneurs take pride in their startup's space. (See Appendix E for snapshots of spaces that symbolize the seven dimensions of successful startup cultures.) A warning to founders who want to rely upon incubators or accelerators, such as Mass Challenge or the Harvard Innovation Lab, to host their startup companies in shared space: It is very hard to develop a distinctive culture embedded in so much public space. Several startup founders in the research sample chose to move out of shared space as soon as they could. Coworking centers such as Regus and WeWork are somewhat better. They provide more private space for startups, but, as CC's Goodman says, "there's no substitute for having your very own space."

Fred Shilmover, founder of InsightSquared, feels that space is a critical contributor to his startup's culture. "Not having private offices has a great leveling effect. That's what our millennial engineers expect . . . but to be honest, I hate not having my own office." He yearns for Insight Squared to have its own building. "I would really like to have our open-office design include outdoor space. All of us like to hang together, and it would be cool to be able to be outside when the weather is warm. Unfortunately, I often have to spend more time with my team here than I do with my family, so the physical environment is important to me."

Diane Hessan is a great fan of the Boston Red Sox. She built a large, open-meeting area called "Fenway Park" into Communispace's headquarters, and insisted that employees use the space for quick get-togethers and collaborative work. In addition to collaboration, Fenway symbolized the company's openness and commitment to having fun.

For entrepreneurs who are thinking about designing, upgrading, moving, or otherwise changing the physical space that their startup occupies, here are a few space tips aimed at reinforcing each of the seven dimensions that were most prevalent in successful startups.

A Sample of Startup Space Tips

Passion

- In the lobby or on the walls, feature photos with short (one or two sentence) stories about how the company saved the day for key customers.

- Have open areas where employees can easily and comfortably gather to listen to the startup's leaders generate excitement for the company's mission.

- Display the mission or vision statement in a prominent open space where everyone can see it, including all visitors.

Ownership

- Have workstations that can be easily moved and regrouped so that temporary teams can be together physically to work on a project.

- Allow people to own their own workspaces by encouraging lots of personalization and avoiding a one-size-fits-all policy.

- Celebrate individual and team accomplishments with testimonials posted on the walls or sides of workstations.

Learning

- Have plenty of white boards, chalkboards, or flipcharts around the office and on common area walls so that people can meet and record their brainstorming ideas.

- Have public gathering places with comfortable chairs so that groups of employees can have informal discussion and learning places.

- If possible, have samples of the product available and visible around the space so people are encouraged to continuously think about new ideas for improvement.

- Have more private and quiet—but still open—space for individual learners to work in.

Collaboration

- Have lots of conference rooms and places where people can easily meet to work together, separate from their regular workspace.

- Have space where employees can eat together without feeling uncomfortable and make sure these spaces are inviting and available as close to 24/7 as possible.

- Make sure that there is plenty of communication technology in all the conference rooms so that collaboration is easy across offices and geographies.

Messiness

- Don't worry about crowded space, or about keeping offices, tables, and work areas superneat (but make sure they are safe and sanitary).

- Treat space as a scarce commodity; encourage people to share work areas, desks, and computers.

- Have the startup top team's workspace match the spontaneity and messiness of the rest of the office.

Transparency

- Eliminate as many solid office or conference room walls as possible and substitute glass walls.

- Post lots of performance metrics—especially those that celebrate customer or marketplace successes—in high-visibility areas.

- Have the startup leaders "close" to all the other employees with a minimum of barriers or status symbol differences.

Caring

- Have space for informal play and recreation, including space for kids and dogs.

- Make sure the kitchen area is big, open, and well stocked with food and drink.

- Dedicate wall space to celebrate community activities with pictures and stories of employees who contribute to causes and projects outside of normal company events.

Systems and Processes

In the very beginning, most startups have few formal systems or processes. The founders and their startup team know what's important, what work has to get done, and who is going to do the stuff that matters the most. There are usually no job descriptions or organization charts. Project plans are written on white boards where they can be easily updated—or even erased. Passion is the dominant feeling at this stage, and Messiness is not only tolerated, but also encouraged, as people jump from one important task to another.

This kind of informality and fluidity can last for weeks, months, or even years, depending on the circumstances: the type of business, the stage of the technology, the availability of resources, and the founders' need for order and control. Sooner or later, customers and investors will mandate that the startup introduce more and better systems and processes. Expenditures need to be more carefully tracked, pricing decisions need to be rationalized, costs and margins measured, and people's responsibilities need to be clarified and better coordinated. The introduction of systems and processes that inhibit and restrict the freewheeling norm of most early stage startups can have a profound effect on the culture. Rippleshot's Tran says: "Our culture had to change from the Wild West to a more disciplined work environment. We needed to focus more on execution, not just invention. We had to spell out individual accountabilities. I knew that this was going to impact our culture, so I had to be very careful. It came down to a matter of balance, and I think we achieved that."

Here are six ways that entrepreneurs in the research sample preserved the essence of their startup culture while introducing new systems and processes:

- Think about it early on. Simple decisions, such as keeping track of work hours, can change a culture in an early-stage company.

- Let people own any new software development process. Engineers create processes as a matter of course. The key is to have it be *their* process.

- Tell them the why behind the system change and people will accept it more readily.

- Don't be heavy handed. Treat any new work rule more as an experiment so you can be flexible and open to modifying rules that people find overly controlling.

- Lead by example. If you want less Messiness, the leaders have to clean up their own act, too.

- Pick the most obvious things that require guardrails and formal procedures. Don't start with shit like a dress code . . .

Perhaps the most delicate—and culturally significant—systems change a startup CEO has to make as his company grows and adds more and more talented (and ambitious) people is defining and clarifying roles and responsibilities. Thiel reflects on his PayPal experience and has this advice for startup CEOs:

> *The best thing I did as a manager at PayPal was to make every person in the company responsible for doing just one thing. Every employee's one thing was unique, and everyone knew I would evaluate him only on that one thing. I had started doing this just to simplify the task of managing people. But then I noticed a deeper result: defining roles reduced conflict. Most fights inside a company happen when colleagues compete for the same responsibilities. Startups face an especially high risk of this since job roles are fluid at the early stages . . . and internal peace is what enables a startup to survive.*[3]

He is pointing to another culturally significant process that startup founders and CEOs will have to deal with as their business expands: performance management and rewards. Although a significant number of startups in the research sample offered employees "a piece of the action" via stock options or equity, shorter-term financial rewards and recognition are always important motivators. For startup CEOs, the cardinal rule when it comes to any performance management process is that it must be perceived as fair. Informal conversations ("you're doing a great job" or "clients love your responsiveness") are fine in the beginning. But informal recognition will eventually have to give way to a more formal appraisal and reward system. And here is where a culture of Ownership, Collaboration and Learning can morph into second-guessing, jealousy, or even backstabbing. Diane Hessan put this issue front and center: "Making sure that the right people—the high performers—were the ones that were recognized at Communispace was always going to be an important part of my job. As you grow, you will have to have an HR function and more formal reward policies and practices. But the CEO needs to have the final word and needs to make sure that people feel they are all being treated fairly."

Metrics

There is an old saying in business that "what gets measured gets managed." This applies in a powerful way to the formation of a startup's culture. On the one hand, if founders care deeply about the quality of the customer experience, they will create and communicate a battery of metrics that measure the quality of the customer experience. On the other hand, if founders feel that the quality of the company's software and technology is the source of their startup's competitive advantage, they will measure all aspects of software performance. And in either case, the entire organization will know immediately what's important and what really counts. The key metrics that are referred to and used by the startup's leadership team define success. They also define the culture.

Dan Lyons, in his book, *Disrupted*, wrote about his experience at HubSpot. As a journalist, Lyons joined HubSpot to create higher-level journalistic content related to inbound marketing that would attract more customers. His number one tool was the HubSpot blog, and he introduced higher quality content. However, his boss, a person Lyons identifies as "Wingman," was totally motivated by a metric called "conversion rate." Here is how Lyons reports it:

> *Wingman has decided that we need to end this kooky experiment with smart content and go back to what works: really basic stuff, the kind of thing that people who know almost nothing about the Internet would be likely to search for on Google. Basically, Wingman is arguing in favor of making the blog dumber. It's fascinating, in a perverse way. Wingman has one goal: to get leads. If our software analytics were to indicate that our best conversion rate comes from publishing a blog post that just says the dogshit over and over again . . . then Wingman would publish that post. Every day. Three times a day. Twelve times a day, if the software said twelve works better than three. Wingman isn't a bad guy. He's just a guy who has a number to hit.*[4]

Lyons takes HubSpot to task on any number of fronts (He labels it "The Happy!! Awesome!! Start-Up Cult"), but his point about the company's fixation on lead generation provides would-be entrepreneurs with a cautionary message about the important role metrics play in defining a startup's culture.

The prevalence and perceived importance of certain metrics not only help to define a startup's culture, but the reliance on metrics and hard data to make key decisions and evaluate individual and group performance can also be a source of strong cultural norms. ezCater's cofounder and CEO Mallett feels that her company's "insanely helpful" culture stems in part from she and her cofounder Briscoe Rodgers' emphasis on being "measurement driven" when it comes to managing people. "We rely on facts. When the metrics and data say XYZ is the way to go, it's hard for people to argue. Our 'objective culture' makes ezCater a psychologically safer place to work, and that makes it so much easier for people to let go of positions they once held and move on."

Rituals and Symbols

Another source of a startup's culture can be the rituals and symbols that founders invent and use to move their organizations forward. Think of rituals and symbols as "the way we do things around here" or "what we always do to run the business." They are the traditions that move the business forward.

When Tribe Dynamics' Begley started the company with only five employees, he initiated what he called "scrum meetings" each morning. These meetings have continued to this day (the company now has over 40 employees). Scrums only last for 20 minutes (from 9:30 to 9:50), but they provide people with an opportunity to get the latest updates, share information and, as Connor says, "recharge people's batteries."

Anthony Rodio, CEO of Your Mechanic, has several symbolic activities that he is using to change his company's culture from its top-down, autocratic beginning. He has everyone attend a "stand-up meeting" every Monday to set goals for the week. He gives out what he calls "peanut awards" to reward employees for "keeping their noses down" and staying focused on getting important jobs done on time and within budget.

Joshua Summers also has rituals that he uses to reinforce the clypd culture: lunch-and-learns each Thursday, Friday demos of software improvements, and the delivery of personally written birthday and anniversary cards to all employees.

Rapid7's Thomas holds monthly town hall meetings where he shares "the good, the bad, and the ugly" with all the startup's employees. As Corey emphasizes: "We value transparency, and these monthly sessions are meant to model that value."

FlipKey's Mahony took pride in a ritual he calls "the Fat Joe project," where non-customer care employees are forced to handle customer complaints so they learn to accept and respect the roles others play in the company.

Such rituals and symbols signal to startup employees what norms, values, and behaviors are important. They help to shape a startup's culture and often have long-lasting affects on what people experience in these companies. But an overemphasis on rituals can make the culture feel too much like a cult or too much like kindergarten, as in "now it's nap period and then we will all get together for circle time." This may turn off some people. The point is to have a limited number of rituals and symbols to reinforce one or more of the seven cultural dimensions characterizing successful startups that can increase a sense of commitment and belonging. Peter Thiel says it again:

> Entrepreneurs should take cultures of extreme dedication seriously. Is a lukewarm attitude to one's work a sign of mental health? Is a merely professional attitude the only sane approach? [T]he best startups might be considered slightly less extreme kinds of cults.[C]ults tend to be fanatically wrong about something important. People at a successful startup are fanatically right about something those outside it have missed. [5]

External Influences on Startup Cultures

Founders and the people they hire are the most important source of a startup's culture. But there are four influences on startup cultures that are only indirectly controllable by the founding team. They are outside of the startup, not inside.

1. Geography

The first external factor that plays a significant role is the geographic location of the startup. There is no better place to start a company than California's Bay Area. (It used to be Silicon Valley, but San Francisco is now equally exciting.) The Bay Area has an amazing startup ecosystem. Stanford spews out entrepreneurs and engineers; so does Google. This means that there is a large, ambitious, sophisticated pool of technical talent. And high-tech talent in the Bay Area moves around—there is no shame in jumping ship. There are also plenty of lawyers, accountants, mentors, and other professional advisors who are used to working out of coffee shops with tiny companies whose ideas are much larger than their pocketbooks. And there is a ton of money, much of it recycled—successful Bay Area entrepreneurs are constantly reinvesting their winnings in new startups. The Bay Area has more venture capitalists per capita than anywhere else on the planet.

Put these all together and you have an outside culture that is more supportive of six of the seven dimensions of a successful startup culture than anywhere else. In the Bay Area, the intensity of the competition for high-tech talent—and the length of time that startups have been blossoming there—have led entrepreneurs to embrace and implement a step-level elevation of the sense of Ownership, Learning, Collaboration, Messiness, Transparency, and Caring in their companies. These cultural dimensions are clearly regarded as a source of competitive advantage. Passion is the only dimension that is equaled in other geographies. New York, Boston, Chicago, Austin, Tel Aviv, Mumbai, and Shanghai are great places to start a new venture. But there is no place like the Bay Area.

Over 20 years ago, AnnaLee Saxenian, now a dean and professor at the University of California, Berkeley, wrote a book called *Regional Advantage*, in which she compared the ecosystems of Silicon Valley and Route 128 in Massachusetts. Despite similar histories and technologies, these two geographic areas spawned quite different kinds of startup cultures. In Silicon Valley, high-tech startups adopted open networks of communication and exchange. Engineers often changed firms or quit their jobs to start new companies. In Massachusetts, leaving a company was viewed as disloyal, so talent tended to stay put. Silicon Valley startups collaborated with one another, often sharing information and resources. Employees of different firms frequently attended the same business and social gatherings. By contrast, even early-stage Route128 companies strove to be vertically integrated and employees had far fewer interfirm interactions. If Silicon Valley's culture was open and fluid, Route 128's was secretive and self-contained.

What Saxenian observed in the 1990s still holds true, although the New York, Chicago, and Boston startups in the research sample are good examples of recent efforts to open up and improve these local entrepreneurial ecosystems. They still have a ways to go, as illustrated by a comment from Greg Besner, founder of New York startup CultureIQ: "The people here in the East are the same as on the West Coast. It's just that out there the engineers move around more. It's hypercompetitive and there is less loyalty." He concludes by remarking "I've never had one of our engineers quit." Although this isn't the case with CultureIQ, when loyalty is celebrated more than innovation or entrepreneurship, the dynamism of the ecosystem can suffer.

2. Industry Forces

The nature of competition, availability of critical resources, level of price sensitivity for its products, degree of customer loyalty to existing offers, and perceived degree of switching costs also can impact a startup's culture. For example, if a startup's technology is radically new and different, what's called "first-mover advantage" becomes superimportant. This means that speed to market, cutting edge innovation, and the rapid adoption of its technology has got to be stressed. And this, in turn, means that successful startups will have cultures that are messy, experimental, demanding, and product-centric. Rigorous cost control and expensive marketing are not going to be a priority. On the other hand, if the startup's success formula emphasizes building great customer relationships and high levels of customer service, successful cultures will be more outwardly focused and place a higher value on going the extra mile to solve customer problems.

The bottom line is that the most successful startups have cultures that fit with the industry forces the company must deal with. Founders and CEOs are best served when they pay close attention to these forces, communicate them to their employees, and adopt practices that allow the startup to respond in a way that ensures growth and profitability. Due to the dynamic nature of industry competition in most high-tech markets, the number one cultural priorities are Learning, Ownership, and Transparency. Although all seven dimensions will usually come into play, these three dimensions tend to stimulate both agility and resilience—strategic necessities in fast changing industries.

3. Technology and Talent

Technology influences everything. Of course, the state of technology for software, AI, data science, and other high-tech startups has a profound impact on their internal culture. It drives hiring decisions, resource-allocation decisions, the emphasis placed on innovation, the value and role of various functions (i.e., engineering versus sales versus customer service, etc.), and all sorts of assumptions startup founders make about how they are going to achieve success in the marketplace. But, even the manufacturing, finance, healthcare, and food and beverage startups in the research sample relied on technology to produce, support, or market their products and services.

Perhaps technology's biggest cultural impact is on the talent that startups require to be successful. The more a startup depends on maintaining a differentiated technology, the greater its need for top-notch engineering or data-science talent. And the greater the demand for such talent, the higher the expectations of talented technology gurus will be. In the Bay Area, almost all the entrepreneurs in the research sample admitted that competition for technical talent was intense and expensive. Ron Croen has a prescient VC's perspective: "For a long time here in the Bay Area, geeks ruled the roost. It was an engineering-driven environment, dominated by Intel, defense firms, and so on. Facebook and social media changed that. Media, apps, and social media are now dominant. We are going back to deeper engineering and science. Ph.D.s are valued again."

"If your culture isn't really, really attractive and compelling, you will never be able to recruit and retain the engineering talent you need," says Takt's CEO Christian Selchau-Hansen. This means that startups, in addition to offering hiring bonuses, equity, and hefty compensation packages, must have cultures that stress Ownership, Learning, and Caring.

Although not as competitive as the Bay Area, the technology and talent challenge dominates startups in Tel Aviv, New York, and Boston. Erez Nahom, founder of KonnecTo, a Tel Aviv data-analytics startup, says, "Finding and keeping software developers is my number one issue." Zac Sheffer, founder of Elsen, a Boston fintech startup, echoes Nahom's concern. So does Michael Tardif, founder of Sourcetop, a New York software development startup: "Affordable software talent is hard to find in New York. I've had to reach out and outsource work to Brazil, Pakistan and Bangladesh." As of mid-2017, these startups were too small to have faced the kind of cultural challenge described by Croen and Selchau-Hansen, but if they continue to grow, they soon will.

4. Funding Sources

Where a startup gets its funding can help define its culture. Self-funded startups and their founders are far less restricted in molding the company's culture than startups that are funded by outside investors, especially VCs. Angel investors have varying degrees of influence, depending on how hands-on they are. Venture capital investors must answer to two constituencies: the companies they invest in and the VCs limited partners (LPs). For better or worse, most VCs pay more attention to their LPs, and often place demands on startup CEOs that impact the culture. For example, Rich DiTieri's Startup Institute changed its strategy from one emphasizing growth to one emphasizing profits. According to DiTieri, this pivot was not his preferred strategy, but it was preferred by the company's largest outside investor. This required a reduction in staff and a refocusing of the leadership team's priorities, both of which drastically changed the startup's culture.

Not all VCs have a negative impact on the seven dimensions that characterize the cultures of successful startups. Brent Grinna, founder of EverTrue, credits Bain Capital with being a powerful advocate of the startup's mission of helping educational institutions raise money. According to Grinna, Bain provided timely financial, as well as community, support.

The right outside investors can also be a source of culture consulting. Eric Paley, managing partner of Founder Collective, a seed-stage fund located in Boston and San Francisco, takes great pride in his and his firm's sensitivity to startup cultures. "We encourage, but don't force startup leaders to invest in the 'soft stuff.' But our experience is that if the founders of the company don't make their company's culture a priority right from the beginning, we'll be in trouble. It's really hard to turn around a startup culture that's gone wrong." When asked what he looks for to tell when a culture has "gone wrong," Paley asks three questions:

- Is the startup's turnover high? High turnover, he knows, is either due to poor recruiting or people leaving because they disliked the work environment.

- Is there ego-driven conflict when the top team meets? Paley looks to see if there is genuine questioning (a good thing) or constant debating (not so good).

- Is the startup's leadership team overly homogeneous? Paley feels that entrepreneurs who only hire people who look and act like them will limit the flow of valuable new ideas.

What's the net? Startups are living organisms, and cultures evolve from a huge number of factors, some of which leaders can control and others they must simply understand and deal with. However, all three sources of culture—people, space/processes/rules of the road, and external influences—could end up being pivotal. Being intentional about a startup's culture is an enormously important task. The notion that your written values statement (or culture code) *is* your culture, or your website *is* the culture, or the schedule of pizza parties *is* the culture, is wrong. The pizza, especially, represents a very small slice of the startup-culture pie.

CHAPTER 5

Creating Your Culture
from Scratch

Before You Start

"CREATING A CULTURE from scratch is one of the greatest satisfactions of entrepreneurship. To do it right, you have to think about it before you start, and you have to be very, very deliberate." So states Shorelight Education's Tom Dretler. Many—but not all—startup founders share Dretler's perspective. Approximately 40 percent of the entrepreneurs in the research sample admitted that they had not paid much attention to the future culture of their startup before they launched their venture. The vast majority of this 40 percent were first time founders. For these entrepreneurs, success was defined in terms of product performance, market acceptance, and the availability of seed capital. Even for more experienced founders, culture is seldom mentioned as a critical component of their initial success formula. Few angel investors or VCs see even a single page devoted to culture when they look at the business plan (or pitch deck) that entrepreneurs use to promote their startup.

This is unfortunate. For, although culture may not destroy a startup with five or six employees, *culture creation starts on day one*. And the entrepreneurs in the research sample, especially those who had started multiple businesses, are adamant that the quality of a startup's culture would very quickly become a critical success factor. In the beginning, the culture is largely in the founders' hands. The sooner the founder (and his or her founding team) can think through and decide on the kinds of feelings and experiences they want their employees to have, the better. How do you do this? Where should you start?

You should start by looking in the mirror. You should ask yourself over and over again, Why the hell am I trying to start and build this new venture? Appendix B is a Founder's Self-Assessment. Use it. One of its most significant parts is in the beginning of the assessment, where it asks you to examine your goals and your motives. There is one fundamental issue that founders need to confront as soon as they get the itch to be an entrepreneur: the wealth versus power dilemma. And here, academicians can provide as much insight as the research sample.

The University of Southern California's Noam Wasserman, formerly an associate professor of clinical entrepreneurship at HBS, authored *The Founder's Dilemmas*, a seminal research-based book on entrepreneurship. He points out that founders need to decide as early as possible whether they are going to try to get filthy rich or try to maintain control of their company. Wasserman's research illustrates that very few founders can accomplish both, and that the sooner they decide how to resolve this dilemma, the better. The founders' appraisal of their fundamental motives for starting a venture will have a profound impact on the startup's culture.

Wealth or Control? Understanding What's at Stake for Startup Founders

Noam Wasserman's *The Founder's Dilemmas* is a remarkably rich source of information about the conflicts, trials, issues, and trade-offs involved in starting and trying to scale a new business. He describes a number of trade-offs that startup founders must deal with. The most fundamental dilemma is the tension between two basic motivations for starting a business in the first place: the desire to build wealth and the desire to maintain control of the enterprise. Of course, almost all entrepreneurs want both. But Wasserman's research shows that few can have their cake and eat it too. Bill Gates, Steve Jobs, and Mark Zuckerman are rare exceptions.

It behooves every startup founder to look in the mirror and try to understand what goal—wealth or power—is personally the most important; each of these motives will determine critically important decisions in building a successful business. Here are brief examples of how the two different motives will lead to two different startup growth strategies.

Looking at the two sets of statements below, which describes how you think you would prefer to build the business?

If your goal is building wealth, you should:		If your goal is controlling the business, you should:
Hire the best possible leadership team, even if it means sharing equity.	*versus*	Look to your immediate network of friends and past colleagues and hire people you are comfortable with as members of your leadership team.
Tap a broad network to find the best possible employees and incent them with cash and equity.	*versus*	Hire employees (from among your family, friends, and past colleagues) who don't require equity or large salaries.

Take outside capital even though it may mean losing a controlling interest in the business.	*versus*	Self fund the business without outside capital; use friends and family loans or rely upon revenue from business operations.
Delegate decision-making authority to members of the leadership team with the appropriate expertise.	*versus*	Keep close control of decision making and build a strong team with you at the top.

Source: Robert Stringer and Kate Merritt

Let's assume you have looked in the mirror, assessed your motives, values, strengths and weaknesses and you still want to start a new venture. You haven't nailed down a final business plan, but you've got a really great idea and you've bounced it off of a few people you trust. They also think it could be a winner. So, you go to work on a product strategy; you make sure the technology works; you start to round up early financing; you decide how you want to go to market; and you develop a lengthy list of all the other things that have to be done before you're ready to take the plunge.

Don't forget to think about the kind of culture you want to have in your new venture. What would a startup culture to-do list look like? You don't have to dot all of the i's or cross all of the t's, but you don't want to wing it. What you need is a prelaunch culture plan: an initial outline of actions and decisions you need to take to increase the probability that your new venture will be successful. Such a plan might be embedded in or attached to an entrepreneur's pitch deck.

Key To-Do's: A Prelaunch Culture Plan

- Get the top team on the same page: Self-knowledge is one of the most valuable assets a founder can bring to a new venture. But before moving forward, make sure that your cofounders, partners, and future leadership-team members are on the same page when it comes to the soft stuff. Having frank and open discussions at this point about personal motives, goals, values, and future thoughts about work norms and policies may seem like jumping the gun, but they will help clarify cultural expectations. Noam Wasserman reinforces the importance of confronting this issue: "Founders tend to neglect these 'soft' factors because they are harder to assess than skill compatibility and functional backgrounds, but they can become serious problems for even the most well-matched teams."[6] (Appendix B can also be used to make sure there is team alignment on the soft factors.)

- Check for commitment to the startup and its mission: Unless the founders share a passion for the startup's mission, and a belief that the venture is worth pursuing with vigor, energy, and personal resources, you are better off not moving ahead—at least not with these partners. No startup culture (or business, for that matter) will succeed without such across-the-board commitment. Richard Rabbat, founder of Gfycat, sums it up this way: "Out here, everyone says that they want to work at a startup, but few people have the courage and maturity to make the commitment that it takes to be successful. Starting a new venture takes a huge personal investment, and you've got to make sure people are willing to make that investment in your venture."

- Plan the physical environment: Space can have a profound impact on the culture of a startup. Chapter 4 reviews many of the possible cultural ramifications of various physical environments. Even before the business is launched, founders should envision and plan for the right kind of working space. Financial constraints may limit the options, but having a plan will be an important guide for your expansion decisions.

- Line up other resources: In addition to the physical space, there will be other resources founders need to hit the ground running with the right kind of startup culture. Think about them. Think about what might get in the way or screw up the work environment in the very beginning. For example: Will you have petty cash and if so, how will it be managed? What kind of computers and technology will work the best and facilitate the communication patterns and habits you want to establish? What goodies do you want to provide to keep the team nourished and motivated during the long working day?

One final warning: Don't try to imitate another startup's culture. There is only one Google, one HubSpot, one PayPal, and one Constant Contact. Many successful entrepreneurs have lots of exposure to other great startups and mentors who can talk about what works in other early stage companies. But the founders in the research sample unanimously agree: Take in all of these data and ideas, but don't follow someone else's culture road map. If you want to build a unique company, build a unique culture.

In the Beginning

Imagine that it's the first day of your new venture. You are confident that your idea and business plan are winners. You've managed to convince a few friends and family members to put up $200,000, which, combined with your own savings, should give you a bit of a runway and allow you to beta test the software and demonstrate its power. You, your cofounder, and the two engineers who have agreed to join you have spent the day in your subleased loft space hooking up your computers, working on projects started during the past few months, following up on a hundred loose ends, calling potential customers and partners, and otherwise getting your shit together. It's 5:30 and one of your engineers says he's calling it a day and going out for a drink. You have a three-page to-do list with lots of unchecked items, and you know that the engineer has a similar list with tons of work that has to be done ASAP. How do you feel? What do you do? What do you say? Be careful. Your culture is at stake.

Once launched, founders' early actions and decisions will have a huge impact on the startup's culture. Whether or not there is an explicit prelaunch culture plan, there are four critical things entrepreneurs should focus on in the beginning:

1. the people who are hired, and the jobs they are expected to do;

2. the rules of the road that are "developed" in the first few months;

3. communication style and messages coming from the top; and

4. the leadership practices of the founding team.

The People and Their Jobs

As outlined in Chapter 4, people are the single most influential determinant of an organization's culture. Almost all of the founders in the research sample said that their initial hires ended up molding the cultural values and norms. And they all had the same advice to future entrepreneurs: hire for motivation and values, not for skills or experience. This is a difficult lesson to follow. However, here are representative comments from successful founders/CEOs:

• "We had five criteria for our earliest hires. Culture fit and values were number one; skills and experience were number five." Conor Begley of Tribe Dynamics

- "From the start, we had to make sure people worked well together, so we hired for IQ and EQ." Bob Gett of Viant

- "My advice would be to start off focusing on hiring the right kind of people—people who love their work and love your company. Passion is much more important than specific skills." Selchau-Hansen of Takt

- "In the beginning, we made the mistake of bringing on people with great trading skills, but lousy attitudes and personalities. It almost killed our culture and our business . . ." Melissa Footlick of TopStepTrader

- "The first four people you hire make all of the difference. Their values and personalities have to jell with yours." T.J. Mahony of FlipKey

This is not to say that founders should hire people just like them. Without a diversity of skills, backgrounds, and experience on the early founding team, the startup may have serious blind spots. The important thing is to build a team that enjoys working together *and,* at the same time, is willing to disagree, challenge, confront differences, and problem-solve in the interest of building a successful business. Founders should also be brutally honest with all of the early new hires. Don't sugarcoat or try to gloss over the realities of your new venture, even if it's struggling. Describe the work to be done, the other members of the team, and the kind of work environment you want to build.

Startups seldom have superclear job descriptions. Therefore, the best kind of early hires should be "athletes" who can pitch in and do multiple tasks and play multiple roles. Successful entrepreneurial leaders make sure that every member of the early team knows what the mission is and what the critical tasks that must be done well are to accomplish the mission. Founders need to establish broad responsibilities, communicate high expectations, and have frequent meetings to review early progress and figure out if individual assignments need to be adjusted.

They also need to consciously create a set of rules of the road.

Early Rules of the Road

So, when that newly hired engineer announces that he wants to take off at 5:30 to go for a drink, what do you do? From day one, founders will have to make a decision about work hours—what time people start work and what time they go home. This may sound trivial, but more than one founder team has split over who works harder, and the importance ascribed to working long hours. It becomes a significant part of any startup culture. Think about it: If you believe in working 80 hours a week, what signal will be sent when a new employee leaves at 5:30? If you think there is an easy answer, consider this: What if this same employee says he has to go home to see his kids? Or what if it's a single mother who wants to leave early to relieve the babysitter? What rules of the road do you want to establish?

Then there is the issue of remote work. How important is it that all your team shows up at the office space? Are you cool with everyone working from home and using technology to communicate, or do you want the physical proximity and serendipity that happens when everyone is in the same space?

Several successful founder/CEOs in the research sample insist that everyone be physically present in the office in order to facilitate collaboration. Former Yahoo CEO Melissa Mayer made an early decision to get people back into the office after years of remote working—a huge and controversial change for the Yahoo culture.

There are many other seemingly small, but potentially significant unwritten rules that should be top of mind for founders. To name a few:

- Dress codes—How sloppy can people's dress be? What impressions will people's dress make on visiting partners, customers, investors, etc.?

- Private space—Will workstations be shared, or will people be encouraged to personalize their space with pictures, plants, food, and mementoes?

- Play times—When will it be okay for employees to stop work and play? After all, there are those Ping-Pong tables . . .

- Cleaning up—Who cleans up the kitchen? Is there going to be a hierarchy of service in the startup, or are employees expected to clean up their own messes? And how much mess will be tolerated?

- Attendance at group events—Are these mandatory? Which ones can someone miss if necessary? Do you want everyone to attend everything even if the event is extracurricular?

- Vacations—Do you expect people not to take vacation even if there is some kind of vacation policy? Are you yourself going to take vacations?

Entrepreneurs with a startup-culture plan will be better equipped to anticipate and deal with many of these early culture-defining rules.

Early Communications

In a startup, communications from the leadership team are amplified in people's minds. The more frequent and open the communication is from the leadership team, the quicker a culture of Transparency will be established. The more the messaging is about innovation and experimentation, the louder the voice of Learning will be. And the more warm and personal the entrepreneur's talks are, the quicker the sense of Caring will arise. Constant Contact's Goodman made it a point to early and often talk about small business customers and this set the tone for the company's customer-obsessed culture.

Successful entrepreneurs do not have to have gilded tongues, but it helps. Words are powerful weapons, so all the members of the startup's leadership team should coordinate their messaging, their emphases, and the tone of their communications. And the pattern of communication should be two-way. There is no quicker way to turn off and demotivate high-powered talent than to talk *at* them rather than talk *with* them. Founders and startup leaders who seem to know it all seldom command the respect that they think they deserve. Most of the CEOs in the research sample emphasize that winning, for them, was a team sport, and one of the most powerful ways to motivate a talented team is to listen to—and listen for—each team member's contribution.

Leadership Practices

In addition to being a very good listener, what other leadership practices are most important in the beginning? The right answer is that *everything* the founders do is important and for better or worse will define the early culture of a startup. But, the entrepreneurs in the research sample point to four leadership behaviors that had a disproportionate influence on their companies' culture:

1. How do startup leaders spend their time? If the founder is a brilliant, introverted engineer and devotes most of his or her waking hours worrying about and messing with the technology and software, the culture will be far different from one with a founder who spends the most of his or her time out in the market talking to potential investors or customers. Founders who spend most of their time with their direct reports or members of their board will create a far different work environment from founders who interact with a broad range of employees, regardless of reporting relationships or status. People will assume that the issues that get the founding team's greatest attention are the most important issues. The lesson is to be conscious of this fact. Solving immediate problems may require lots of top-team time, but startup leaders need to

keep their heads up and balance fire fighting with bigger-picture matters so that the organization and its culture understand what the real priorities are.

2. What metrics are used to measure performance? Successful entrepreneurs always have a dashboard of metrics that they use to evaluate the health of the business they've started. The dashboard is not a private tool. To be effective and useful, the entire startup organization needs to know how success will be defined and measured. As Wayfair's Shah says, "Our culture and our company is data driven and everyone knows the key metrics we use to manage the business." Whether it's new installations, customer complaints, net new revenue, or conversion rate, whatever the metrics are that comprise the leaders' dashboard, they will be used as a scorecard and will be important motivators for the high achievers. And the culture will line up with what people see as the company's success formula.

3. How do leaders handle rewards and recognition? In the beginning, there will be an employment contract—usually unwritten—that defines what people get for working with the founding team in a crazy and exciting new venture. What's the deal that people get for working in your startup? Is it a low salary with lots of equity and thus direct ownership in the ultimate outcome? Is it a moderate salary with lots of other perks like free food and unlimited vacations? How long will the financial rewards be deferred, and what form will they take? The nature of the compensation and rewards "contract" will determine each employee's going-in expectations.

However, these initial expectations will change—sometimes dramatically—depending on how people are treated once the startup gets going. Informal reward and recognition practices often trump the original "contract" when it comes to the culture and to motivating high levels of performance. Here are a few of the day-to-day actions that leaders engage in that could have a big impact on how rewarded people feel and how motivated they are to contribute 110 percent to make your startup successful:

a. Who do you spend time with? Face time with the founder is perceived to be an important positive sign—a reward. Lack of exposure to the leader is the opposite.

b. In those early company meetings, who is recognized and praised . . . and who is ignored? How gets to speak and who doesn't?

c. Who is asked to deal with your biggest customers? Who is brought along to those important sales calls . . . and who is left behind?

d. How are mistakes handled? Are people publicly called out, or are mistakes and missteps dealt with in private and coupled with encouragement?

e. When good things happen, are individuals recognized, or is the emphasis on a team of contributors?

f. How are under-performers treated? How fast do leaders deal with poor performance? How public are the consequences?

g. What decisions do leaders make themselves and what is delegated to others?

4. Some entrepreneurs feel that they have to make *all* the important decisions. Others learn to delegate early and often. Startup cultures of Passion and Ownership and Collaboration require high levels of trust. And that means that the founders and the other members of the top team must be willing to let go of big decisions. Founders who hold on too tightly to decision-making authority will

not only find themselves working 80-plus hours a week, they will become bottlenecks and barriers. This reality is most obvious when a startup is scaling fast, but it is also a critical cultural and business success factor in the beginning. Listen to what Viant's Bob Gett, who is now an angel investor, says about this issue: "A startup culture is always formed in the first 90 days. At Viant, I hired supersmart, highly motivated young men and women and let them figure things out and make most of the decisions. Now, as an investor, I look for entrepreneurs who aren't afraid to empower their people."

Less experienced people will make poor decisions, but the key to success is having a culture that allows mistakes to be quickly corrected. A culture of Messiness instills a sense of confidence and makes it much easier for the business to bounce back from wrong moves or lousy decisions. (See Chapter 7 for more on this topic.)

Creating a culture from scratch is hard work. It requires self-knowledge, forethought, and a great deal of insightful leadership. Don't wing it. The most successful entrepreneurs are intentional when it comes to managing the soft stuff. The least successful fail to think about the culture they want to create. They are then left wondering what went wrong when the best talent leaves, deadlines are missed, customers complain about the attitude of their employees, and the business goes sideways. Having a prelaunch culture plan will help, but no plan—and no planners—will be able to anticipate all the hectic ups and downs of startup life. Keep the seven dimensions of successful startup cultures in mind, along with the advice you have heard from the entrepreneurial leaders in the research sample. Do this, and your chances of winning significantly improve.

CHAPTER 6

Scaling Your Culture— Five Traps to Avoid

WHAT'S IT LIKE to scale a startup? Listen to Communispace's Diane Hessan, who sold the company to Omnicom in the nine figures:

Our early success was largely due to the fact that we spoiled our customers with tremendous service and responsiveness, and we all could back each other up. As we grew, that was impossible and so, maintaining quality was a huge challenge. Our systems were fine for a $2 million business, but not for a $10 million one, or a $30 million one—and people would come into my office, screaming: 'This place is a crazy train!'

It made me furious because from where I sat, sales were soaring and I wanted people to be as excited as I was. I quickly learned that we had to stop the management by intuition we were used to. We needed new metrics and processes, and a way to hire people ahead of the curve so that we had time to train them. And our culture was changing, but we didn't want to lose the inspiration and energy we had in the beginning as a startup.

Everything changes when you scale. And the faster you scale, the faster things change. To maintain the right kind of startup culture, each of the seven dimensions outlined in Chapter 2 may have to morph during scaling as the company grows. For example, scaling a culture of

- **Passion** will require ever more careful screening of candidates to make sure they embrace the company's mission and find working for the company a dream job. The founder may no longer be able to interview everyone, which means that the leadership team will need to be able to both convey passion for the mission and detect it candidates.

- **Ownership** will require that all members of the leadership team delegate important decisions and make sure that even the lowest-level employees can see how their jobs contribute to the company's growth and profitability.

- **Learning** may have to be budgeted more, but mid-level managers especially must continue to expect and reward people who take risks and try out their new ideas.

- **Collaboration** will be more difficult as functions and departments grow and are staffed by new talented employees (who will always want to showcase their individual skills). Casual and informal collaboration will have to be augmented—not replaced—by more regular cross-functional meetings.

- **Messiness** shouldn't be stifled by too many systems and processes, even though more of these will be needed.

- **Transparency** will require more time and effort by the CEO and leadership team, especially as new performance metrics are introduced and communication has to take place with more people (and in different time zones). If it's too expensive to have in-person company-wide meetings, technology may have to substitute for face-to-face interactions.

- **Caring** will become more expensive as new perks and support systems are put in place. It will be necessary to spell out a few new rules and boundaries, but leaders must be careful not to dilute the company's basic commitment to care for all its people.

The key to scaling a winning startup culture is avoiding the five most common culture traps. Founders should focus on the to-do's that will help preserve the fundamental norms and values of the winning startup culture, while adding the resources needed to expand. None of the startups in the research sample had exactly the same experience, but almost all were able to avoid the traps by heeding the to-do's that allowed them to effectively scale their winning cultures.

Culture Trap No. 1: Growth Addiction

Growth is a narcotic for many entrepreneurs. It is a measure of their brilliance, the rightness of their vision, the power of their technology, and their dream of great wealth. However, when a startup experiences explosive growth, some nasty things can happen to its culture. The attributes that proved so attractive and satisfying when the company was small and intimate—even when it was messy and scrambling with an uncertain future—can lose their coherence and validity. As Hessan notes above, driving hard for rapid growth can result in people feeling like they're on a crazy train. The Growth Addiction trap can destroy a winning culture.

As the leader of a rapidly growing startup with a vulnerable culture, there are three ways to avoid falling into the Growth Addiction trap and one recommendation for how to get out of the trap once you're in it.

1. Re-examine Your Growth Strategy

Perhaps the most obvious to-do when important cultural norms are being ignored or violated and people seem to be unable to cope with all of the demands of explosive growth is to step back and analyze the trade-offs being made. Is it necessary to enter this new market when you really don't have the ability to provide after-sale service that is up to your quality standards? With your stretched development resources, do you really need four new products this year? Fearing that you don't have the capacity to do great work, should you take on this new project?

Matthew Price, CEO of cyber-security startup Cloudflare, has this to say about how to avoid the Growth Addiction trap:

> *If you're growing faster than doubling the number of employees in any 12-month period, then inherently you're going to have more new people than old people. And in the short term, maybe that's fine. But the culture can start to suffer because there's nothing foundational to keep you stable. For startups like us, there's constant pressure to grow faster, but if you do that, then there are no culture-keepers of the organization.*

When a startup company's offer takes off and the demand exceeds the company's ability to deliver on its brand promise, the smartest response is sometimes to scale back, not scale up. Not only will a growth pause help to preserve a winning culture, it may help to preserve the startup's reputation.

2. Redefine Your Talent Pipeline

Asking a founding team to slow down the growth of a startup that is proving to be a roaring success is a tough ask. Another way to avoid many of the negative aspects of the growth-addiction trap is to redefine the concept of a talent pipeline. Finding, onboarding, and training new employees to keep up with rapid growth are often the biggest sources of culture strain and pain. Without new talent, the startup's existing staff becomes overworked and stressed out. The feeling of Collaboration, Caring, and even the Passion, can erode. Messiness turns into craziness. How can you get ahead of the need for great talent?

Several of the founders in the research sample adopted an always-recruiting policy. The talent pipeline was no longer defined as a list of candidates for existing job openings. These successful leaders of high growth companies actively searched for great new hires, even when there were no formal jobs waiting for them. These leaders recruited the best and the brightest engineers no matter what, even to the point of telling an outstanding candidate, "We are offering you a job; but, instead of quitting your old job in two weeks, we want to bring you on in three months." If the candidate balked or questioned this rather strange job offer, he or she was asked to contact Mary or Joe or any number of other new hires who had been brought into the rapidly growing startup this way. Invariably these references were positive—partly because the Growth Addiction trap was being avoided.

3. Hold Ownership Meetings

Another to-do to mitigate the strain that explosive growth puts on a winning startup culture is to call employees together and share with them the realities of the situation. In these meetings, you must share the good news and the bad news. The good news is that the company has gained tremendous market traction and is going to beat all of its growth targets. The bad news is that this is going to mean more work, more demands, and more effort from all employees. Then *ask* the team how they want to deal with this good-bad news reality. For the high achievers in most startup organizations, this is almost a trick question. They will often sign up for the challenge, motivated and buoyed by the opportunity to be part of a winning team in a winning company.

If possible, the leaders should offer short-term financial incentives for the extra efforts in store for employees. And formal and informal social events, celebrations, and other non-financial rewards should also be part of the package. While the Growth Addic be mitigated or avoided by reinforcing and leveraging Ownership in the culture, continual ownership meeting if people don't see that progress being made.

4. Leverage the Culture to Rebound

Falling into the Growth Addiction trap usually leads to a significant performance hiccup, compromising your winning culture. The startup's entire business strategy becomes open to question. Layoffs and unhappy customers are common. Over a dozen of the entrepreneurs in the research sample reported that they had grown too fast and had to dig their way out of this culture—and business— trap. Assuming the fundamental business strategy remains sound, the best path is to leverage what used to be your cultural-success formula. And, even if you determine that falling into the trap warrants a strategic pivot, you will need to leverage your culture to bring it back to where it was.

Let's assume that before your startup crashed, the culture was similar to the winning cultures described in chapters 2 and 3. Here is how you can leverage the seven attributes that define the right kind of startup culture:

- Passion—Get back to basics: Re-emphasize the fundamental mission that created your original passion. As long as your mission still makes lots of sense, stop talking about all sorts of new growth options or initiatives. Invite your most loyal customers to sing your praises and get their message to all employees.

- Ownership—Don't try to turn things around by yourself. Re-engage people in helping you rebuild the company, even if it is in a more scaled-down form.

- Learning—Don't stop focusing on innovation and personal learning, even if you have lost a few talented engineers. Stress the opportunities for those who remain, and challenge them to see what they can do with fewer resources.

- Collaboration—This aspect of the winning culture may be sorely tested as people worry more about their own jobs than the historical emphasis on sharing and collaboration.

The to-do for startup leaders is to visibly reward high collaborators and stress the fact that collaboration is the best way to do more with less.

- Messiness—This attribute may have to morph. As long as those closest to the mess don't become too focused on process rather than flexibility and speed, some reduction in informality is good.

- Transparency—This is one of the most important aspects of a startup's culture to leverage. A frank and open discussion of the consequences of falling into the Growth Addiction trap will reinforce Ownership, and it will help to rally people around the rebuilding strategy. Transparency will be even more important lever for the new top team to use if falling into the Growth Addiction trap has led to a change in the startup's leadership.

- Caring—Leveraging this cultural dimension is all about taking good care of any employees who were laid off or let go. Generous treatment of former teammates, including help in finding new jobs, will send the reassuring signal that the startup's caring culture has not been abandoned, even when its growth hit the wall.

Culture Trap No. 2: Ego Trip

Not many of the entrepreneurs in the research sample succumbed to the Ego Trip trap, but it can be a common stumbling block for startups. Stated simply, this trap is all about founders or CEOs who don't let go. They are hard working, talented, and often inspirational. But they try to do everything. They are the chief engineer—or they insist on having the last word on any and all software changes. They are the chief strategist—sometimes refusing to accept bad news coming from the market. They are the chief salesperson—and want to be in on all customer calls and pricing or delivery decisions.

Armed with supreme self-confidence, they are often doomed to fail because their egos prevent them from delegating and creating a sense of ownership in the minds of others. As described in Chapter 2, Your Mechanic's Anthony Rodio had inherited a broken startup culture because the original founders were autocrats who had fallen into the ego-trip trap. There are only three ways to avoid—or get out of—this culture trap:

1. Recognize the Symptoms

Because the Ego Trip trap is so personal, it is critically important for the CEO who is at the center of everything to recognize the symptoms of *being in* the trap. Based on the comments of both successful and less successful entrepreneurs, here are just a few of the most obvious signs of trouble:

- You are working way too hard. You find yourself in the office long past when others have gone home.

- You are a bottleneck. Your inbox is overflowing with things that are awaiting your review or approval.

- You can't trust others. You find yourself doubting others' ability to make the right decision or execute something up to your standards (even when they are considered the best and the brightest).

- Your leadership team is reluctant to make decisions. Your top team members are spending way too much time in your office double-checking decisions that are clearly within their scope of authority.

- Lousy top team meetings. Your direct reports seem always to be arguing with you, or worse, they no longer are forcefully expressing their opinions.

- Your schedule is crazy. You are expected to be two places at the same time, and your calendar is so full that you no longer have any private or downtime.

2. Look in the Mirror

For ambitious entrepreneurs, ego trips—even if the symptoms become clear—are exacerbated by a failure to keep in touch with one's personal limits and shortcomings. To be successful and avoid the Ego Trip trap, founders should spend more time looking in the mirror. This is a critical to-do *before* founders take the plunge and start a new venture (the self-assessment tool in Appendix B can be very useful here). And it is an important to-do as the startup begins to scale. Having a candid conversation with oneself is tricky. Therefore, the best way to look in the mirror is when someone else is holding it up while participating in the candid conversation.

Who should a struggling startup CEO turn to? First, if you have a spouse or personal partner, talk things through with them. You may be surprised at how obvious it is to them that your ego is a barrier to the success of your business. Second, find a mentor or professional associate you can talk to—one who is familiar with your business situation, as well as your personal ambitions. The best mentors are found outside of the company, because they will have few, if any, mixed motives about helping you. Knowledgeable board members are often a great source of leadership advice. Seeking candid feedback on your leadership is really valuable, even if you fear openly admitting you are in an Ego Trip trap. The symptoms detailed above will most likely be visible to your board, so being proactive in discussing them will enhance, rather than jeopardize, your relationship with the board.

Last, there are a number of programs, consultants, and educational experiences that can help executives who are in the Ego Trip trap.

3. Hire a Chief Operating Officer

The other to-do that was suggested by the entrepreneurs and VCs in the research sample was for the founder or CEO trapped by being the center of everything—trying to do too much—to immediately go out and recruit a rock star number-two leader to act as the startup's COO. This is can be viewed as a drastic (and usually expensive) fix, but it can be a godsend. Finding the perfect number-two executive is easiest if the founding team has openly discussed the startup's leadership and governance practices. Not surprisingly, a founder or CEO struggling with the Ego Trip trap often ends up appointing or recognizing an existing member of the leadership team as his or her COO.

It took David McCue, founder of the McCue Corporation, several tries over several years to find an executive he trusted enough to delegate significant responsibilities to. Because he was such an exceptional leader, the company's growth slowed while he searched for a COO, but it never lost its momentum. McCue finally ended up promoting one of his longest serving executives to the position.

Culture Trap No. 3: Taking Culture for Granted

One of the most important traps to avoid if the startup is to scale and be a real winner, is taking the culture for granted. Paying attention to culture is one of the bedrock lessons of *Culture.com: How the Best Startups Make It Happen*, and when founders take their startup's culture for granted, the chances of building a really successful business are significantly reduced. The mad scramble for customers and resources may mask any culture faults for a while, but sooner or later the cracks will appear: low morale, turnover, disputes between workgroups, customer-service glitches, or generally poor performance. Even at HubSpot—a very successful company, now public, with a powerful and distinctive culture—Chief People Officer Burke admitted that until it opened its office in Dublin, Ireland, the main focus was on growth and not the culture: "We had to stop taking it for granted, and [cofounder] Dharmesh Shah assumed responsibility for increasing our focus on culture. He conducted many rounds of employee interviews and we came up with a long deck all about the HubSpot culture code."

Company cultures are living organisms. Every new employee, every strategic pivot, every customer crisis, and every new product development will influence the culture. In smaller startups with scarce resources, and larger than life leaders, these influences tend to be magnified. Therefore, even when the venture gets off to a great start and develops a winning culture that has all of the seven attributes described in Chapter 2, the culture is not "nailed;" it is not "set;" it is not "done." It can *never* be taken for granted.

There are five relatively straightforward to-do's to avoid the Taking Culture for Granted trap, and while most of them have been explained already, the underlying importance of a healthy culture in determining the success of a startup warrants summarizing them here:

1. Create a Prelaunch Culture Plan

Chapter 5 describes the guts of such a plan, but the most important action is to imagine the future, to think about what your company will be like when it has 40, 50, or 100 employees. How many customers or offices will you have? What will the expanded management team look like? Lay out your ideas for scaling the culture just the way that you would plan for your future cash flow. Involve all the members of the founding team and make sure to iron out any disagreements about the norms, values, and practices that you hold dear and want to emphasize.

2. Document the Culture

Documenting a winning culture is a great way to make sure that the culture isn't taken for granted. Detailed techniques and advice about how and when to document a winning startup culture can be found in Appendix C. Just the *process* of trying to write it down will help to solidify the key messages and reinforce its value as a management priority. It will be important to treat the culture statement as a living document; periodically revisit and update the document with employees if you want to make sure people appreciate its importance and relevance.

3. Appoint a Culture Committee

At some point, many of the founders and CEOs in the research sample formed what they often called a "culture committee." Sometimes (for example in the cases of Rapid7 and Viant) the committee was just one person. But usually it is a small group of employees—not including the founders—who volunteer and who meet regularly to reflect upon and discuss the company culture. Often this kind of committee has a budget to sponsor social events or culture-building activities. And, in startups such as ReviewTrackers (a rapidly growing company that markets online review management software to enable its customers to measure their customers' experience), in Chicago, the committee conducts frequent employee surveys to gather data about the culture and make recommendations to the senior team about how to keep the winning culture alive and well.

4. Leverage the Culture in Times of Crisis

As mentioned in the discussion of the Growth Addiction trap (Culture Trap No. 1), almost all startups have crises. They hit a wall—whether it's overgrowth that can't be handled, a product that fails, a customer that leaves, an investor who backs out, or a market that disappears because of some unforeseen political decision. When faced with a crisis, successful startup leaders—in addition to scrambling to get back what was lost—leverage their company's culture. That's why so many founders of successful startups say that culture trumps strategy. Having a culture that is resilient and allows the company to quickly recover and bounce back from a crisis is a priceless asset.

The best startup leaders know this and try to leverage their winning cultures, even when struggling to regain their company's momentum. For example, when the State of Illinois stopped paying its bills, ThinkCERCA was owed a ton of money and hit a wall. The company had to lay people off. But Abby Ross, ThinkCERCA's CEO, celebrated the company's customer-obsessed culture in an all-hands meeting and re-emphasized the importance of serving the needs of teachers, no matter what Springfield's politics were.

When clypd hit the wall, it was because one of its major customers discovered that the clypd software didn't work as promised. Even though clypd's Summers knew that the company was going to lose money, he decided to invest whatever it would take to correct the mistake. The company worked overtime for 45 days to fix the problem. Summers admitted that they all had a "hangover" for six months because of the effort required, but he used the experience to put clypd's culture that emphasized Caring into perspective: "I don't think we could have asked people to do what they did if we didn't have the kind of culture we had."

5. Put Culture on the Agenda

Scaling a startup will stretch all aspects of the business, including its winning culture. VCs, angel investors, and startup board members point to their appreciation of the role that culture plays in the long-term success of almost all startups. Therefore, founders and CEOs should make sure to put culture on formal meetings' agendas with these influential people. Once in the habit of involving these influential players in discussions of non-numbers topics, it will be much harder to take culture for granted. Smart investors and board members will see to that.

Culture should be on the agenda at every board meeting. Culture should be part of every investor update. Culture should be mentioned when you're raising money in an A-round, B round, or other financing event. And culture should be a topic discussed at every offsite—even when the primary purpose of the meeting is only tangentially related to the soft stuff. Automatically putting culture on agendas will keep it front and center and that's how to avoid the Taking Culture for Granted trap.

Culture Trap No. 4: Misplaced Loyalty

Perhaps the most important resource needed to scale any business is talent, and several of the most common culture traps involve finding, keeping, or getting rid of talented people. The Misplaced Loyalty trap is all about getting rid of talented people who are no longer performing. There are two versions of this culture trap. The first is failing to let go of a friend or partner who helped you start the business. The second is failing to get rid of a high performer who violates the winning cultural norms that have been established.

Many entrepreneurs—especially those who have high needs for control of their new venture—start off by working with friends. Friends are the most comfortable partners for startup founders. Of course, founders in the research sample also say that these friends "must have the right stuff." What exactly constitutes the right stuff in the mind of successful entrepreneurs? Complementary skills and experience? A shared commitment to the startup's mission? A personality and value system that is 100 percent congruent with the founder's? Access to important resources, technology, or customers? All of the above? Other things?

And this is where the first version of Culture Trap No. 4 can begin. Most startups pivot, shift, and change in hard-to-predict ways as they scale. Skills that were absolutely critical on day one become less so as the venture matures. The easy partnership and sense of common purpose can become strained as new demands are placed on the company and its leaders. New talent with new expertise can sometimes place the original experts in a secondary role. And, when the startup grows and adds lots of people, leadership practices (rather than loyalty or functional skills) become a much more important factor in determining the success of the business.

Founders who remain loyal to the partners and people who were originally part of the startup team—even when it is clear that they no longer can handle the increased responsibilities and complexity that come with growth—fall into the trap of Misplaced Loyalty. Founders may hate to admit that their friend or partner isn't cutting it. They think about all the *past* contributions this person has made to the success of the business, rather than focusing on the needs of the *future*. And they often kid themselves into believing that no one is noticing this misplaced loyalty. They don't see the impact on the culture: the lowering of performance standards, the dilution of Transparency and Ownership, and the abrogation of the Learning dimension of the culture.

Brent Grinna, the original founder of EverTrue, admits that he almost fell into the Misplaced Loyalty trap twice. When he wanted to scale his startup, he realized he couldn't get the required funding unless he had a heavyweight technical partner and a really good social-media expert. So he brought on two other cofounders. After several years of explosive growth, EverTrue's technical staff expanded exponentially: "After a while, it became clear that the high-powered technical partner, who was a terrific doer, didn't much care for being a manager. It was really tough to part ways, but he's moved on and is doing great." With the other cofounder, the Misplaced Loyalty trap was avoided in another way: "We were able to keep him—although he was also too small for the expanding marketing role—by hiring people over him . . . and he's cool with his new role."

The second version of the Misplaced Loyalty trap—failing to get rid of a high performer who doesn't fit the culture—is just as tricky as the first version. As the startup ramps up and has to rapidly add to its talent pool, it is not uncommon for unique technical expertise to be overvalued. Possible cultural shortcomings can be downplayed during the hiring and onboarding process, in hopes that the performer's technical contribution will make up for any rough edges. (Review Chapter 5 to learn how to minimize your talent-screening mistakes.) But, people seldom change their personalities and the rough edges will ultimately force leaders to make a choice: tolerate the disruptive behavior or eliminate it in the interest of reinforcing the norms of the winning culture that you want to preserve.

Disruptor Beam's Jon Radoff describes falling into the second version of the Misplaced Loyalty trap and he labels it "a culture moment":

We had a very talented Star Wars *product manager who was an autocrat. He thought that he was the only one who could innovate. We place an emphasis on one-on-one feedback and coaching here, so I spent a lot of time trying to work on the situation with the* Star Wars *team, but I finally had to fire him because he couldn't empower or motivate the team. In retrospect, I should have done it much sooner. After he left, the* Star Wars *innovation performance*

*increased dramatically. Today, it's even clearer that 'talented
assholes' don't fit in the Disruptor Beam culture.*

Avoiding the Misplaced Loyalty culture trap is not easy, but there
are four to-do's that if followed will minimize the likelihood of falling
into it:

1. Implement More Rigorous Up-Front Screening—This
    to-do works best for avoiding the second version of the
    Misplaced Loyalty trap. The Founders Self-Assessment
    in Appendix B-1 and the prelaunch culture plan outlined
    in Chapter 5 are also good tools to help founders and
    early members of the startup leadership team to sort out
    possible future culture conflicts. Again, Chapter 5 also
    speaks to the up-front talent screening process.

    If you still have culture fit questions but the pressures
    of scaling the business require you to quickly recruit
    specialized talent, consider bringing the talent in on a
    temporary basis. This will put explicit boundaries on any
    loyalty feelings and provide both you and the new hire a
    trial period to test the fit. It will make parting much easier
    if it becomes necessary because of a culture conflict.

    Last, founders should avoid signing employment
    contracts or giving up-front incentives, options, or equity
    if there is *any* question as to the candidate's ability to fit
    with your winning startup culture. Such arrangements
    add a legal dimension to the loyalty issue and only add to
    the difficulty of avoiding the misplaced-loyalty trap.

2. Have Candid Early Conversations—The second to-do is
    to engage in early conversations about the importance of
    your startup's culture and your expectations for everyone's
    behavior and adherence to the rules of the road. (See
    chapters 4 and 5 of this book for more about them). Here
    is another instance where a prelaunch culture plan can be

a very useful tool and conversation platform (again, see Chapter 5). There is no payoff for avoiding or delaying candid discussions about a person's observed behavior if it appears to be in conflict with the kind of culture you want, even when it is one of your closest friends who seems to have forgotten the startup's culture guidelines.

Startup leaders who value the company's winning culture should not be deterred from addressing a person's out-of-step behavior even when it comes to them second-handed. If the source is a trusted one, the wise startup leader will confront the issue with the offending employee and point out that his or her performance is *always* going to be evaluated based on the brilliance of the work *and* the style with which the work is carried out. This is relatively easy in small organizations where there are few places to hide. It's harder as startups scale.

Rapid7's Thomas points out that it is often the case that the founders of a startup can lose touch with what's going on with frontline people when the company grows larger and more geographically dispersed. When Rapid7 hit $20 million in revenues (with over 75 employees), he hired Christina Luconi, an experienced human resources professional, to "watch over" the culture. Together, they developed a unique strategy to avoid falling too far into the Misplaced Loyalty trap. As Christina relates: "Last year, we had three top-flight engineers up for promotion. They were individually really talented, but I learned from their managers that they were lousy collaborators. That's a strong cultural priority here, and I trusted what I was being told. So, we *provisionally* promoted them. They had six months to change their behavior. And it worked."

3. Document the Culture and Use the Document to Discuss Performance—Documenting a winning startup culture not only helps avoid Trap No. 3 (Taking Culture

for Granted), it also can help address the Misplaced Loyalty trap. The more employees in the organization understand and accept the standards against which their performance will be measured and evaluated, the harder it will be to hide or ignore cultural missteps. As the business scales, new hard performance metrics will be developed and used. Performance metrics for the soft relationship and cultural standards are much harder to establish, but they also have to be developed and used. Without a written cultural statement that says what's important, performance discussions with otherwise high-performing technical or functional employees could devolve into arguments. It's not at all helpful to be forced to talk about the desired attributes of the culture in vague or ambiguous terms. Even worse would be to fall back on the weak I-know-it-when-I-see-it threshold test for unacceptable behavior.

The best way to avoid either version one or two of the Misplaced Loyalty culture trap is to document the kind of startup culture that you feel is integral to your company's success formula and use the document as a performance-management tool. As outlined in Appendix C, a written cultural statement is particularly helpful when it not only describes values, but also describes what those values look like in action on the job.

4. Use an External Coach or Mentor—Many of the successful entrepreneurs in the research sample say that they avoided a number of potential pitfalls and culture traps by having a mentor or personal coach. Highly successful startup Pixability's Bettina Hein credits her coach with helping her avoid early-on missteps. CC's Gail Goodman often relied on a peer group of other entrepreneurs to be a sounding board. Diane Hessan used a personal coach for several years to help her scale Communispace. So did Jules

Pieri, founder of The Grommet. TopStepTrader's entire leadership team used the Junto Institute. And ClearSky Data's Ellen Rubin's most pointed advice for would-be entrepreneurs is: "Have mentors. Startup leaders need a sounding board, and outside mentors are much better able to speak the truth and be helpful than insiders."

One excellent source of cultural advice can come from the startup's investors or board of directors (see Chapter 5). These people have a vested interest in the entrepreneur's success, and often have the wisdom and perspective to provide unbiased advice not only about avoiding the Misplaced Loyalty trap, but also most of the other traps.

A Final Tip for Scaling a Winning Startup Culture: Keep the Founders Involved

Almost all the entrepreneurs, angel investors, and VCs in the research sample say that the founders of a successful startup have to be there to scale a winning culture and avoid falling into culture traps. Wayfair's Niraj Shah was emphatic about this point: "The key to scaling a winning culture is remaining *founder led*. It's leaders who create culture, and no leaders are more important than the founders."

HubSpot has successfully scaled most aspects of its culture, but Burke admits that it takes a lot of time and effort: "In the beginning, the way to build a startup culture is by *doing*. When you grow as fast as we have, you build the culture by *teaching*." That's why cofounder Dharmesh Shah spent all that time documenting the culture. Burke points out that Brian Halligan, HubSpot's other cofounder, continues to be involved personally in supporting the HubSpot culture code, although he can no longer interact with every employee: "We've grown, and Brian can't walk all of the halls like he did in the beginning. We just have too many halls."

Eric Paley, one of Boston's most successful VCs, sums up the importance of having the founder personally involved in scaling the startup's culture: "If the founder doesn't make culture a top priority when the startup scales, we—as early investors—are likely in trouble. It's so much harder to change a culture once it has deteriorated."

CHAPTER 7

The Payoff—Having a Winning Culture

IT IS MUCH easier to build a successful company when its startup culture is a winning one from the very beginning, and the founders are smart and skilled enough to make sure that, although the culture will morph, it never loses its basic characteristics and values. Turning around and fixing a broken culture is hard to do, even with the best of intentions. Broken cultures cannot be hidden. Customers will notice a decrease in service and responsiveness, bugs in the software won't get fixed, and the startup's high achievers will start to leave the organization or they will be looking for new jobs. Recapturing the enthusiasm, energy, and unvarnished commitment of the early days will require a new kind of leadership—one that is up to the task of changing people's expectations and work habits.

Hard as it is, it can be done. The key is recognizing that the culture is broken and needs to be fixed—and then having the courage, resources and competence to rebuild it along the lines described in this book. Think back to the dilemma that Andy Hunter faced when he realized that his firm's investment in DataBracket was about to be wiped out because of poor startup leadership and a resulting sick culture. Eight months after the Venture Capital Partners meeting described in this book's Introduction, Andy Hunter was able to smile again.

The Rest of Andy's Story

A Different Kind of Meeting

Andy Hunter was smiling as he squeezed into his chair at the end of the large table in Venture Capital Partners' conference room. It felt good to no longer be the center of attention. When it came around to his turn to update the VCP partners on the progress and status of the firm's investment in DataBracket, Andy spoke with confidence. The Power Point slide that was on the screen in the front of the room was entitled *B ROUND*.

"Well, as proof that DB has turned it around, we are pretty solid in soft circling all of the investors needed for the $5 million B-round. I think firm commitments will be coming in next week, once we nail down the details of the term sheet. I don't see any major issues there. Half of our bridge loan will be paid off and the other half will be rolled into equity at the new valuation. Ever since we replaced Kelly and a couple of the bad apples at DataBracket, they've been cooking with gas."

John Heuser, VCP's managing general partner, interrupted Andy with a shit-eating grin on his face: "Your choice of Stan as the new CEO and bringing in Kate as CFO were both spot on. A lot of eyebrows were raised in the market, but I think your forcefulness with the board and with Kelly made all of the difference. And Stan seems to have re-energized Charlie Argenti and his whole engineering team. The software is singing, and almost all the old customers have returned. I understand that we've also seen a couple of those hot-shot engineers who jumped ship last year boomerang back to DB. Not bad. Andy can breathe again because our early-stage portfolio is now in good shape." Everyone around the table was smiling.

As Andy ran through the numbers and the terms for the proposed DataBracket B-round of financing with the VCP partners, he couldn't help but reflect on the last eight months of work with DB. Once the full board saw how bad the startup's culture was, Kelly was out. Nobody thought he was capable of radically changing his leadership style, and everyone agreed that a radically new kind of leadership was required. Stan Phillips was an experienced entrepreneur and he proved his mettle as a turnaround CEO in his first month by getting rid of DB's mediocre CFO and replacing him with Kate Halpern. Kate seemed to be a calming influence, especially with the other investors. Surprisingly, Phillips did not replace DB's other cofounder, and Kate soon became Charlie Argenti's 'best buddy' on the DB leadership team. Stan, Argenti, and Kate came up with a more focused development plan that was eagerly accepted by the DB sales force. Four months into his tenure as CEO, Stan started to see rapid growth again.

Andy's fellow partners warmed up to the topic and a lively discussion ensued. It was John who finally asked the question on most people's mind: "So, Andy, what's the story with Charlie Argenti over there at DataBracket. You told us last year that he was a loser as a leader. *Tone-deaf* I think was the term you used . . ."

Andy was ready for John's question because they had spoken about it on a number of previous occasions: "I was wrong on that one. All Argenti really cared about was the technology and the data. As soon as he got out from under Kelly, he actually relaxed a little. He stopped being a jerk with his people and regained his old confidence—I refuse to call it *swagger*. Anyway, the customers still love him. I guess another lesson we all learned from the DB experience was to give people a second chance once you've changed the leadership at the top."

Lessons Learned

Because he thought that every VCP partner could learn something from his almost disastrous experience with DataBracket, Andy ended his 10-minute review of the proposed financing with a slide titled Why Culture Counts. Here are its bullet points:

- To understand the culture, look hard at the founder or CEO
- Ask to see the company's plans for scaling its culture
- Stay on top of the soft stuff—look for clues things aren't right
- Listen to employees and customers
- Step in fast—leverage our board position

Final Thoughts

Culture.com: How the Best Startups Make It Happen is filled with anecdotes, guidelines, tips, quizzes, and examples to help would-be entrepreneurs and their advisors figure out how to create and sustain the right kind of culture in a startup organization. There is no way to capture all of the possible takeaways, but the research that went into this book—a review of what other experts have written about culture, the Harvard experiments, and the face-to-face interviews—lead to several salient recommendations about how to make great startup cultures happen.

First, founders should pay attention to culture from the very beginning. People's experience—the working definition of culture used in this book—starts on day one. The work environment has a huge influence on human motivation. Therefore, *founders must be intentional about the work environment they create in their company.* In many cases, culture is just as important as the business strategy, the technology or the customer experience. There are probably startups that have grown and enjoyed success without a winning culture. But they are the exception, not the rule. It may not be immediately obvious to observers of new ventures, but behind the scenes, building the right kind of culture provides a startup with a tremendous long-term competitive advantage.

Second, there is no perfect startup culture. *Some combination of the seven characteristics or dimensions in Chapter 2 will be the key to a startup's success.* Would-be entrepreneurs, advisors, and founders who are wondering how to best tap into the motivational energy of their people should carefully consider what the best startups have done to create and scale winning cultures.

Third, leaders create cultures. Founders and CEOs need to concentrate on their values and cultural priorities as much as they do their brilliant technology, product, and delivery system ideas. *Startup leaders shape the culture from day one,* and they are always in the spotlight. Therefore, they must be visible and articulate about what they expect, what's important to them, and what will not be tolerated when it comes to work practices, social behavior, and interpersonal relationships. As the company grows, leaders must not lose touch with their role as caretaker of the culture.

Last, *the best startups make it happen because their leaders take advice from others who have been there before.* They have mentors and advisors. They learn by doing, but are open-minded about listening to the counsel of other entrepreneurs. They are not know-it-alls, and they are not defensive when it comes to trying out new leadership approaches or practices. That is why the messages and lessons related in this book will save you a lot of heartache and money.

APPENDIX A

The Research

THE RESEARCH FOR *Culture.com: How the Best Startups Make It Happen* is divided into four buckets. Bucket No. 1 contains what is often called "library research," a review of a sample of the published readings and writings on startup culture. Bucket No. 2 holds the research and laboratory experiments conducted at The Harvard Graduate School of Business Administration in the 1960s and continued at The Forum Corporation, Harbridge House, Inc., and at Mercer Delta Consulting in the 1970s, 1980s, and 1990s. (See *Leadership and Organizational Climate*, Stringer, 2002). Bucket No. 3 consists of the content analysis of the published culture codes from 26 startups and early-stage companies. Bucket No. 4 is the most salient and details the author's first-hand experiences, in particular, interviews and conversations conducted with over 100 entrepreneurs and venture-capital investors.

Bucket No. 1: What's Been Written About Startup Cultures?

A lot has been written about corporate culture, but very little about startup cultures. Up until 10 or 12 years ago, writers focused on understanding and explaining the cultures of large, complex organizations.

Many of the books and articles about startups have something valuable to say, but almost none of them explicitly consider in depth the topic of how to create and scale a winning culture. Publications called "guidebooks" tend to focus on the economics of startup-business models—how to raise money, how to leverage technology and the Internet, and the best go-to-market strategies. The few that do discuss culture seem to take it for granted, providing only general tips for would-be entrepreneurs, such as "be transparent" or "don't punish mistakes." The most interesting publications tend to be the personal stories of successful entrepreneurs and their experiences building a single (usually wildly successful) company. But it's very hard for an entrepreneur with a handful of colleagues, a new idea, and no money to relate to Peter Thiel's PayPal story or Ben Horowitz's experience with Opsware, although both Thiel and Horowitz do provide useful insights about the soft side of startup life (see Thiel, 2016, and Horowitz, 2014).

Prior to the recent books that try to deal with startup culture, perhaps the foremost expert on corporate culture is Edgar Schein of MIT's Sloan School of Management. Schein has written extensively about all sorts of organizational cultures and grad-school entrepreneurs are sometimes pointed to his work, especially his book with the inviting title, *The Corporate Culture Survival Guide*. Although he is certainly a brilliant commentator and an expert on large-company cultural dynamics, his perspective on startup cultures is surprisingly sparse (see Chapter 7, "Culture Creation, Evolution, and Change in Start-Up Companies" in Schein, 1999[1]). This stems from the fact that Schein wrote his books before the dotcom era and based his conclusions on his exposure to, and consulting experiences with, large companies. His case studies and observations about startups are quite limited and are all based on retrospective analyses and secondhand information.

In spite of the lack of broad-based startup culture literature, authors like Horowitz, Thiel, Lyons, David Rose, Bob Dorf, and Steve Blank have insights that the author found useful to support (or question) the conclusions stated in this book. Appendix A-1 outlines the first bucket of research writings that formed a subset of the frameworks and conclusions referred to in *Culture.com: How the Best Startups Make It Happen.*

Bucket No. 2: The HBS Climate Study

In the late 1960s, foundational research on motivation and organizational climates was conducted at HBS. This research, described in detail in *Motivation and Organizational Climate* (Litwin and Stringer, 1968), demonstrates that different work environments (called "climates" not "cultures") arouses different kinds of motivation and leads to different kinds of behavior and organizational performance.[2] The HBS research was funded by a grant from the General Electric Company and was aimed at the cultural impact on the three powerful intrinsic social motives: Need for Achievement, Need for Affiliation, and Need for Power. The Need for Achievement was of special interest.

Renowned Harvard University psychologist David McClelland published *The Achieving Society* in 1961. In it, he labeled the Need for Achievement (nAch) as the entrepreneur's motive, and described achievement motivation as the driving force behind entrepreneurial activity. His 1962 article, "Business Drive and National Achievement," was the most popular *Harvard Business Review* article that year (measured by requests for reprints).

To understand the importance and relevance of nAch to the study of startup cultures, let's look at the definition of this motive syndrome as described by George Litwin and I for The Forum Corporation[3]:

The Need for Achievement (nAch)

Need for Achievement is the need for measurable personal accomplishment. People who have high achievement motives seek out challenging or competitive situations and have realistic goals and high standards. There are five themes that indicate high nAch.

1. **Out-performance of someone else**... *winning is important; so is demonstrating that you can do a better job than someone else.*

2. **Meeting or surpassing a self-imposed standard of excellence**... *high-quality work is valued whether or not it involves competition with others; high achievers seek to find better methods of doing the work.*

3. **Unique accomplishment**... *accomplishing something other than an ordinary task; being an innovator.*

4. **Establishing long-term life goals**... *high achievers have long-term expectations for themselves; they are ambitious.*

5. **Plans for overcoming obstacles**... *thinking and planning for the future by trying to anticipate any obstacles to achieving his/her goals.*

Need for Achievement is what makes most startup founders and those who are attracted to and thrive in startups tick. Startups are magnets for high achievers. A startup culture that stimulates and reinforces nAch is going to generate a tremendous amount of innovation, risk-taking, persistence, commitment, and energy.

The HBS experiment successfully created a climate that aroused nAch and statistically demonstrated that organizations that featured high levels of aroused nAch outperformed the head-to-head competition in the same industry. During the study, three companies were formed and they were "in business" in HBS classrooms during the summer of 1965. All of the companies were building radar machines and towers with Erector Set parts. Each of the companies was managed and led specifically to arouse one of the three social motives: the British Radar Company to arouse the need for power, the Balance Radar Company to arouse the need for affiliation, and the Blazer Radar Company to arouse the need for achievement. At the conclusion of the experiment each company, in fact, had different climates and the target social motive was successfully aroused.

According to almost all the performance measures, Blazer Radar—focused on nAch—won the day.

Litwin and Stringer described the elements of the high-achieving climate created at Harvard as follows[4]:

Climate Dimensions that Impact the Need for Achievement

1. **Structure**: *the sense that things are carefully spelled out and well organized, including an emphasis on hierarchy and status. This dimension tends to decrease nAch.*

2. **Individual Responsibility**: *the feeling that you can work without lots of supervision or double-checking, that you are in control of your work and your results. This dimension will arouse nAch.*

3. **Support**: *the existence of positive helping relationships aimed at getting encouraging effort. This dimension has a moderate arousal effect on nAch.*

4. **Rewards**: *the sense that rewards—both formal and informal—are performance-based. This dimension will arouse nAch.*

5. **Conflict**: *the feeling that conflicts are confronted and out in the open, as opposed to avoided or compromised away. This dimension tends to arouse nAch.*

6. **Standards**: *the establishment and communication of high performance standards and expectations. This dimension will always arouse nAch.*

7. **Risk**: *the sense that moderate and calculated risk-taking is encouraged and rewarded. This dimension will always arouse nAch.*

These climate dimensions closely parallel the culture dimensions identified in the third bucket of research. But as you will see, there are important differences.

Although the HBS experiment was a dramatic success, with 20/20 hindsight, it didn't capture the full implications of the research and how relevant it would become to the study of startup cultures in the 21st century. The researchers didn't call Blazer Radar a startup, but that's exactly what it was. Back in the 1960s, HBS was just beginning to be interested in entrepreneurship, and startups were not of major interest. GE funded the research to focus entirely on large, complex organizations and their work environments. For example, at the end of the book that reported the HBS work, here's what was said about the high achievement climate[5]:

> *Achievement-oriented climates appear to be appropriate in areas that demand individual initiative and calculated risk taking (as in many sales organizations and some applied engineering departments). Such climates would also be appropriate in any organization seeking to grow rapidly in a changing environment, where individual responsibility and risk taking are inevitably required.*

(See Litwin and Stringer, 1968,189)

Bucket No.3: Analysis of Startup Culture Codes

Appendix A-3 provides a list of the startups and early-stage companies that have published culture codes. These decks describe the core values and themes of 26 successful companies. A careful content analysis of all 26 reveals the most dominant cultural norms listed below in order of how frequently each was mentioned.

1. Learning/Innovation
2. Transparency
3. Collaboration/Sharing
4. High Quality
5. Humility/Lack of Ego

6. Ownership

7. Caring

8. Fun

9. Messiness/Comfort with Ambiguity

10. Customer Focus

11. Grit/Doing More with Less

12. Passion

Bucket No. 4: Personal Experience and Interviews

In the late 1990s, the cost of acquiring and using digital technology plummeted and a new world of dotcom startups was born. Economic activity and commentary since that time have been dominated by the likes of Apple, Google, Amazon, PayPal and Uber. What role does culture play in a "unicorn?" What is it really like to work in an early-stage company whose playbook relies so much on technology?

The Research Sample

Appendix A-2 provides a list and description of the 100-plus companies in the research sample. As you can see from this Appendix, most of our startups are in the United States, many in the Boston area, but others are dispersed in other cities and countries. Over 80 percent of the startup sample was technology driven, and almost all considered software engineering, data management, or digital expertise as a vital function. Women founded 25 percent of the sample companies, and the average age of the entrepreneurs was between 30 and 33. Most interestingly, almost half of the sample was first-time founders; three dozen were second-time founders and the rest had started three or more businesses prior to the one that was studied.

What Data Was Collected?

As is made clear in Appendix A-2, a number of the companies and entrepreneurs included in the research sample were businesses that were part of the author's investment portfolio. Data collection from these startups was informal and consisted of coaching and mentoring conversations. These discussions ranged over a wide variety of cultural issues, including the founder's leadership and organization-building strategy, the search for talent, and the importance of building a high-achieving culture.

In 2017, a more formal data-collection process was begun. One- to two-hour interviews were conducted with the CEOs or founders of over 50 startups. These interviews covered a series of straightforward issues and questions about the dynamics of each startup's culture. For example:

- Does culture matter?
- If so, what role does it play in your success formula?
- What is the culture in your company like?
- How did it get that way?
- How is your culture maintained, reinforced, and managed?
- Other than yourself—as the founder or CEO—who else has influenced your company's culture? How?
- What are some do's and don'ts for startup founders and CEOs when it comes to culture?

Although most of the interviews were only with the CEO/founder, on several occasions one or two other members of the leadership team were included. To validate and expand upon the culture conversations that were conducted with the CEO/founder, there were follow-on group meetings with employees of several of the startups. There were a few new war stories that came out of these focus groups, but in none of the employee meetings were the comments, stories, or observations about the culture significantly different from what was learned from the CEO/founder. Two things may be concluded from this: (1) As is clear from the description of the dimensions of a successful startup culture, this sample of successful startups proved to be remarkably positive and transparent organizations, with few hidden agendas or fractious conflicts, and (2) successful startup cultures are almost cultlike and the members of these organizations know, recall, and relate very similar stories and experiences.

APPENDIX A-1

Library Research Books

The Corporate Culture Survival Guide (Jossey-Bass, 1999)	Edgar H. Schein
Zero to One (Crown Business, 2014)	Peter Thiel
Organizational Culture and Leadership (Jossey-Bass, 1985)	Edgar H. Schein
Disrupted: My Misadventure in the Startup Bubble (Hachette Book Group, 2016)	Dan Lyons
The Hard Thing About Hard Things (Harper Collins, 2014)	Ben Horowitz
Motivation and Organizational Climate (Harvard University Press, 1968)	George H. Litwin and Robert Stringer
The Startup Checklist (Wiley, 2016)	David S. Rose
The Startup Owner's Manual (K&S Ranch, Inc., 2012)	Steve Blank and Bob Dorf
Hot Seat: The Startup CEO Guidebook (O'Reilly Media, 2015)	Dan Shapiro

Startup Upstart: The Evolution of Idea to Company (CreateSpace Independent Publishing Platform, 2012)   David Cummings

The Startup Survivor (Golden Oak Writers Guild, 2017)   Michael Maloof

The Lean Startup (Crown Business, 2011)   Eric Ries

Leadership and Organizational Climate (Prentice Hall, 2002)   Robert Stringer

The Achieving Society (Van Nostrand, 1961)   David McClelland

Intrinsic Motivation (Plenum Press, 1975)   Edward L. Deci

Drive (Riverhead Books, 2009)   Daniel H. Pink

Corporate Cultures (Perseus Books, 1982)   T.E. Deal and A.A. Kennedy

Regional Advantage (Harvard University Press, 1996)   AnnaLee Saxenian

Organizational Climate and Culture (Jossey-Bass, 1990)   Edited by Benjamin Schneider

The Founder's Dilemmas (Princeton University Press, 2012)   Noam Wasserman

APPENDIX A-2

List of Startups and Venture Firms in the Research Sample

- 18 Rabbits (California)
- Adjoint (Boston)
- Advanced BioNutrition (PA)
- Affinnova (Boston)
- Bamboo Tori (New York)
- BioVittoria Ltd. (China)
- Boathouse Sports (PA)
- Boston Logic (Boston)
- Boston Seed Capital (Boston)
- Broga (Boston)
- Caaapital, S.p.A. (Mexico)
- Cambio Coffee (China)
- Catalant Technologies (Boston)
- ClearSky Data (Boston)
- ClickR (Boston)
- clypd (Boston)
- CoachUp (Boston)

- Comentis (CA)
- Communispace (Boston)
- Constant Contact (Boston)
- Cortex, MCP (CA)
- CultureIQ (New York)
- Data Point Capital (Boston)
- Disruptor Beam (Boston)
- EdBridge Partners (New York)
- Edible Ventures (Boston)
- Electro Optical (New York)
- Elsen.co (Boston)
- Enabling Healthology (PK)
- EverTrue (Boston)
- Evoqua (New Jersey)
- ezCater (Boston)
- Feel Good Foods (New York)
- FlipKey (Boston)
- Flying Spark, Ltd. (Israel)
- FORKY (Greece)
- Founder Collective (Boston)
- Frostimo (China)
- GaGa's Inc. (Rhode Island)
- Gezlong (Turkey)
- Genius Juice (CA)
- Gfycat, Inc. (CA)
- Greenbean Recycle (Boston)
- Halo Neuroscience (CA)
- Highfive, LLC (CA)

- HubSpot (Boston)
- Immaculate Baking (Boston)
- Insight Squared (Boston)
- Instinct Health Science (Boston)
- Izze (CA)
- Kedallion (New York)
- KonnecTo (Israel)
- Learn Launch (Boston)
- Little Duck Organics (Texas)
- MassChallenge (Boston)
- McCue Corp (Boston)
- New Life Solution (Boston)
- NurtureMe (Texas)
- One Key Ventures (Chile)
- Outcome Health (Chicago)
- Outside the Classroom (Boston)
- Peach (Boston)
- Pixability (Boston)
- Privy (Boston)
- Pro Hoop Strength, LLC (Texas)
- Rapid7 (Boston)
- Real Food Solutions (Boston)
- ReviewTrackers (Chicago)
- Rip Digital (New York)
- Rippleshot (Chicago)
- Scientific Nutrition Products (Boston)
- Scioko (China)
- Sequoia (CA)

- Shoebuy (Boston)
- Shorelight Education (Boston)
- Smart Lunches (Boston)
- Sonoma Beverage Works (CA)
- Sourcetop (New York)
- Starry (Boston)
- Startup Institute (Boston)
- Sundial Brands (New York)
- Takt (CA)
- The Community Roundtable (Boston)
- The Davis Companies (Boston)
- The Grommet (Boston)
- The Water Initiative (New York)
- The Welcoming Committee (Boston)
- ThinkCERCA (Chicago)
- Top Shelf Cloths (New York)
- TopStepTrader (Chicago)
- Tribe Dynamics (CA)
- Veggie Fries, Inc. (Boston)
- VetCentric (New York)
- Viant (Boston)
- Vsnap (Boston)
- Wayfair (Boston)
- WeDecide (Turkey)
- Whole Health (Ohio)
- Wise Owl Holdings (New York)
- Your Mechanic (CA)
- Zappos (Nevada)

APPENDIX A-3

A Select List of Growth Companies Published Culture Codes

- Asana (San Francisco, CA)
- Baremetrics (Birmingham, AL)
- Big Spaceship (Brooklyn, NY)
- Buffer (London, England)
- Clef (San Francisco, CA)
- Disqus (San Francisco, CA)
- Doubledutch (New York, NY)
- Etsy (Brooklyn, NY)
- Genius (Brooklyn, NY)
- GitHub (San Francisco, CA)
- GitLab (San Francisco, CA)
- Grammarly (San Francisco, CA)
- Handy (New York, NY)
- Hootsuite (Vancouver, Canada)
- IDEO (Palo Alto, CA)

- Nanigans (Boston, MA)
- Next Big Sound (New York, NY)
- Percolate (New York, NY)
- Rainforest (San Francisco, CA)
- Redmart (Singapore)
- Robin (Boston, MA)
- Spotify (Stockholm, Sweden)
- Tettra (Cambridge, MA)
- Thoughtbot (Boston, MA)
- Uberflip (Toronto, Ontario)
- Zaarly (San Francisco, CA)

APPENDIX B

Diagnostic Tools

One of the prerequisites for success as an entrepreneurial leadership is self-awareness. This was emphasized in Chapter 5 as an important starting point and as a way to avoid the culture traps described in Chapter 6. In this Appendix there are two easy-to-use diagnostic tools to help you assess your readiness to be a startup founder and—if you've already jumped into the startup game—to assess the strengths and weaknesses of your current company culture.

These are by no means the only helpful diagnostic tools available to entrepreneurs. CultureIQ, a startup in its own right founded by Greg Besner in 2013, has a number of excellent culture-assessment technologies that would-be or current entrepreneurs can access (go to cultureIQ.com).

Questions about how to best leverage the following diagnostic tools should be directed to: Bob@crimsonseedcapital.com.

APPENDIX B-1

Founder Self-Assessment

Introduction

Self-awareness—knowing what you want, knowing what you're good at, where you need help, and what's really important to you—is a critical part of a successful entrepreneur's playbook. The sooner founders understand the personal dynamics that will be in play in their startups, the sooner they will be able to develop a winning game plan, one that includes the steps necessary to build a unique and rewarding startup culture.

This self-assessment will help you as a founder to clarify your motives, your values, and the kind of environment you want to create in your startup organization. The assessment will focus on four aspects of self-awareness:

1. Motives: Why are you planning to start a new business? What are you after? How will you know that you've been successful?

2. Personal Strengths and Weaknesses: What are your personal strengths and weaknesses as a leader of this new business? Where do you have your proven track record of success? Where might you need the most help?

3. Values: What are your values? Other than the growth and profitability of your startup, what other outcomes will mark you as a success in your own mind?

4. Your Ideal Startup Culture: What kind of work environment turns you on? How do you want the people in your company to *feel* about the culture and the work they do? What are the cultural attributes that will be most important to the success of your startup?

How to Use the Self-Assessment

The most effective way to use this assessment is to walk through it with your cofounder(s) and discuss each of the questions. You don't need to write down the answers, but it will be helpful to take notes in order to capture where you and your co-founder(s) are in synch and where you have differences that will need to be resolved.

If you do not yet have cofounders, then talk through the assessment with a mentor, a former colleague, or someone who knows you well in a business setting. Having a self-assessment sounding board will help clarify and confirm your responses.

Motives

1. Why do/did you want to start this business in the first place?

2. What is your vision for the business? What ultimate goal do you want the business to achieve?

3. Most entrepreneurs want to be master of their own destiny and get rich. If you had to choose <u>one or the other,</u> would you want to:

    a. stay in control of your business, or

    b. make a whole lot of money, even if it meant giving up control?

    (See Chapter 5 for an explanation of the possible implications of these two motivations.)

4. If you had to pick *only one* thing that makes you feel good about yourself and gives you the greatest sense of satisfaction, would it be:

    a. accomplishing something that hasn't been done before and requires lots of risk-taking,

    b. being in a position to positively influence people and events, or

    c. being really popular and having great personal relationships?

    (See Appendix A for a discussion of these three motives.)

Personal Strengths and Weaknesses

1. What *specific* career experiences have you had that prepare you for launching this new business?

2. How much *industry and market knowledge* do you have?

    a. Knowledge of customer segments and the unmet needs of each segment?

    b. Knowledge of your potential competitors and the trends that will be driving competition in the industry?

    c. Awareness and detailed knowledge of the products and services that customers will compare your offer to or might act as substitute products?

    d. Knowledge of the pricing strategies competitors are using now and may use in the future?

    e. Understanding of your supply chain—all of the things that go into making your product/service a winner— and knowledge of where to go if a supplier fails you?

    f. Knowledge of and experience with the technologies that are important to your business?

3. Which business functions (finance, marketing, sales, customer service, production, R&D, etc.) are you most experienced in? Least experienced in?

4. How much managerial experience do you have? How many people have you managed at any one time in your career? Do you *like* to manage people?

5. How would you describe your management style? Have you ever received feedback (positive or negative) on your skills as a people manager?

6. Have you worked in a startup/small business before? If yes, what was the most important thing you learned?

7. How wide/deep is your own personal network of business contacts—potential customers, employees, investors, advisors, etc.?

8. What kinds of financial resources can you bring to bear? Your own money? Friends and family money? Other potential investors who know and trust you?

9. Does your personal situation allow you to work 24/7 for the foreseeable future? Will your family and friends emotionally support you in this venture?

Values

1. What are your most important values? How would you like people to describe the real you?

2. Think about a leader you admire—what values does this person seem to exhibit?

3. What do you most value in work relationships?

4. In personal relationships?

5. If you think about the *image* of the organization you want to build, what three to five values would best describe that image?

6. What three to five values should all members of your leadership team share?

Your Ideal Startup Culture

1. When you think about great places you have worked in the past, what are the three to four words you would use to describe how it felt to work there?

2. Think about work environments have been the *least* attractive to you—what three to four words describe how these felt?

3. What is *most important* to you in terms of how you want your startup to feel as a place to work?

4. The following seven topics describe the attributes of cultures of successful startups. Given your goals for the business, and the kinds of people you hope will join your organization, *stack rank* these seven cultural attributes in order of importance to you when it comes to contributing to the long-term success of your venture (1 being the most important, 7 the least).

   After you have done this, think about your management style, your values, and your strengths and weaknesses as a leader, and note which two or three of the seven you think will be the *hardest to sustain* over time and which two or three will be the *easiest to sustain*. If you are unsure, note to be determined (TBD) next to that attribute.

   a. Passion—everyone is super gung-ho and committed to the business

   b. Ownership—people feel empowered to make decisions on their own

   c. Learning—there is a strong emphasis on experimentation and a commitment to innovation

    d. Collaboration—people enthusiastically work together without much hierarchy or silos

    e. Messiness—there is less concern for order than there is for making stuff happen

    f. Transparency—all kinds of business, performance and personal information is openly shared

    g. Caring—all employees feel genuinely supported; the company is a home away from home

APPENDIX B-2

Culture Assessment

This assessment will help you identify the kind of culture you currently have in your startup. It is based on the 7 Dimensions of Successful Startup Cultures described in Chapter 2.

Instructions:

- Respond to each item using the scale below, and put the appropriate number in the box to the right.

- Sum the scores for each dimension.

- Then plot your dimension scores on the chart at the end of the assessment so you can see your culture pattern.

- Finally, answer the three questions at the end to capture your conclusions about your culture, and what, if any, changes you may want to make.

Culture Assessment Scale—The statements below are true . . .

1=Never   2=Occasionally   3=Sometimes
4=Often   5=Always

PASSION

1. People talk about how proud they are of the work
    we do to their friends and to each other.

2. Around here, employees go the extra mile to get
    things done, even if it means givi ng up weekends or
    staying late at night.

3. People here believe strongly that what we are trying to
    accomplish as a business is important and valuable.

4. Employees pitch in and even do tasks they don't like
    if it furthers the company's mission.

5. Everybody here works to the max—nobody
    slacks off.

                                              Total Score

Culture Assessment Scale—The statements below are true . . .

1=Never   2=Occasionally   3=Sometimes
4=Often   5=Always

OWNERSHIP

1. Around here, people make decisions on their own—
   they don't have to wait for the go-ahead from someone
   higher up.

2. Employees worry about the finances of the business—
   they're very careful with the company's money.

3. People here feel personally responsible for each
   customer's experience and level of satisfaction.

4. If employees think a task is critical for the business,
   they will take the initiative and just do it.

5. People here are constantly looking for ways to
   improve the business, even in areas that are not part of
   their job.

Total Score

Culture Assessment Scale—The statements below are true ...

1=Never   2=Occasionally   3=Sometimes
4=Often   5=Always

LEARNING

1. Around here, people are encouraged to try new things, even if it means mistakes will happen.

2. Leaders here spend time actively coaching people and helping them learn and grow.

3. We use company time to share new ideas and new approaches—and everybody participates.

4. Our company is known for hiring the best and the brightest—and we take pride in keeping ourselves up to date on the latest developments.

5. Employees are expected to work actively to learn new skills and develop their own capabilities.

Total Score

Culture Assessment Scale—The statements below are true . . .

1=Never   **2=Occasionally**   **3=Sometimes**
4=Often   **5=Always**

COLLABORATION

1. People here pitch in when they see someone else needs help, even if it's not their job.

2. Our space is laid out so that people can easily gather to meet, discuss ideas and work on problems together—and we encourage that.

3. Around here, if you have a good idea, you can just speak up; everybody's opinions are respected.

4. We put teams together based on the best people for the job, not based on titles or job descriptions.

5. When people have issues with other colleagues, they deal with them directly, with no backbiting or gossip.

Total Score

Culture Assessment Scale—The statements below are true . . .

1=Never   2=Occasionally   3=Sometimes
4=Often   5=Always

MESSINESS

1. When people here are faced with obstacles, they find creative workarounds to get the task done.

2. We're writing the "rule book" as we go along— employees are expected to create new procedures and processes if there aren't any already in place.

3. People around here are good at adjusting and changing the way they do things—just as long as they get the job done.

4. Employees are OK with doing more with less—they like finding ways to solve problems even with limited resources.

5. We don't have actual job descriptions here—people jump from task to task depending on what's most important.

Total Score

Culture Assessment Scale—The statements below are true . . .

1=Never   2=Occasionally   3=Sometimes
4=Often   5=Always

TRANSPARENCY

1. We have regular and frequent company-wide meetings to share company information—both the good news and the bad.

2. Around here, everybody knows what the standards for good performance are, both individually and at the company level.

3. We regularly post our results against our key performance metrics—there are no secrets.

4. People speak up here—if they have an opinion, even an unpopular one, they are encouraged to share it.

5. Leaders here are open and honest with their employees—there aren't hidden agendas.

Total Score

Culture Assessment Scale—The statements below are true . . .

1=Never 2=Occasionally 3=Sometimes
4=Often 5=Always

CARING

1. Employees often talk about how it feels like a family here—people look out for one another.

2. If people need time off to address personal issues or to recharge, they are encouraged to just do it—we believe personal lives are important.

3. Colleagues really enjoy spending time together, both during work hours and outside the office.

4. Fun is important around here—and we make time to include fun activities as a regular part of company-wide meetings and events.

5. We take time to get to know each person working here as an individual not just as an employee.

Total Score

Summary

Put your total scores for each dimension in the boxes below and then plot these scores on the chart.

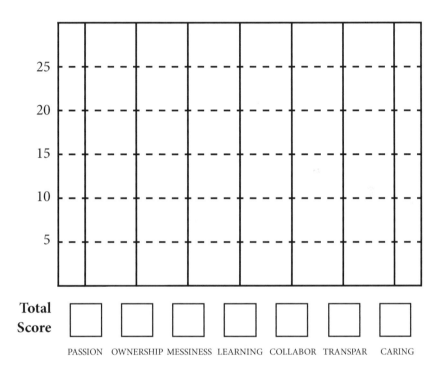

25						
20						
15						
10						
5						

Total Score

PASSION   OWNERSHIP MESSINESS LEARNING COLLABOR TRANSPAR CARING

1. Can you spot any **drawbacks** to your current culture? What are they?

2. Which one or two culture dimensions are the **most important** to your startup's success formula?

3. What **leadership practices** have to change to ensure that your company has a winning culture?

APPENDIX C

Tips for Documenting a Winning Startup Culture

In the beginning, a startup's culture just *is*. As we've discussed, founders who have been there before are much more intentional about articulating what kind of culture they have or they want. First-time founders often aren't. It's almost impossible to successfully scale a winning culture and avoid the common culture traps without documenting it in some form and in some way.

When should a founder write down or document a startup's winning culture? How should this be done? Those startups in the research sample that had been in existence for four-plus years all had written statements or Power Point decks that described their company's culture. Many younger startups also had documented their cultures. Pixability's Hein says it best: "When there were only 10 or 12 of us I was dead set against doing some sort of 'values exercise.' But we were growing fast and I had a mentor who told me that culture happens whether you define it or not, and I should be proactive to describe the culture I wanted. So we developed a 'culture code.' It has become a powerful tool for me and our other leaders. We use it for hiring, performance reviews . . . and I talk about it all the time. Now that we've scaled to over 100 employees, I think it is magic."

There is no one best way to capture the cultural experiences in a startup that is scaling, but here are what you can consider best practices.

Involve a Broad Group of Employees

Entrepreneurs who are self-confident and have strong opinions about the kind of culture they want to have will often simply write it down and assume that will do. Unfortunately, that won't do. As was pointed out in the Introduction, culture is what the people in the organization experience and, no matter how charismatic and inspirational the founders may be, they are not the ones to describe what people experience. So, the way to do it is to involve a broad group of employees and *ask* them to define the most important and powerful elements of the work environment. Whether you call these things "core values" (Communispace) or "principles" (Viant) or "cultural principles" (Catalant Technologies) or a "culture code" (HubSpot and Pixability), the important point is to try and capture what people feel and experience. Niraj Shah admits that he's rewritten the Wayfair core values statement several times—each time involving a broader group of people—to make sure they had a description of the culture that resonated from the top to bottom of the organization.

Stefania Mallett of ezCater originally worked with seven other members of the executive team to draft cultural principles. They came up with 12 items. The executives then went to their teams to see if the 12 were the right things to emphasize and document. The executives reconvened 30 days later to review the broader input. Three items were dropped and three others were changed. The result was called ezCater's Culture Recipe.

Rely on Experience, not Wishful Thinking

If the startup is killing it and you want to document an honest description of its winning culture, have people look backward, not forward. You want to capture the stuff that has generated the most energy and commitment, the stuff that has been the biggest motivator, the experiences that have proven to inspire team spirit and outstanding performance, not what you wish or want it to be like. If the document has all sorts of great sounding words and concepts that have little relationship to what people have actually experienced, it will fall flat. It won't match what current employees know to be the culture; it won't be a useful guide for new recruits; and it won't help you avoid those culture traps.

At Takt, in San Francisco, the founding team has been careful to keep revisiting their original startup culture statement as they scaled the company. It was first drafted when there were only five employees; then redrafted when there were eight; then again when there were 20; and there are now sixty. According to Christian Selchau-Hansen, the description has "morphed," but not changed dramatically. "It's who we are, not some grandiose statement of wishful thinking. And we now use an anonymous employee survey to check to make sure it's still relevant. I think that the *process* of scaling and documenting a culture is almost as important as the *content*."

After three years—many of them characterized by external and internal struggles—Diane Hessan decided to document the Communispace culture. She gathered her top 20 managers in a room and asked them to describe "[T]he kind of company they wanted Communispace to be," Hessan says. She told people to think hard about their past experience in the company—the times when they felt the most motivated and committed—and then had people put their thoughts on Post-it Notes all over the walls.

Try to Capture Stories

Jon Radoff, founder of Disruptor Beam, stated the obvious when he says, "Words are not the culture. It's what people feel and do that's the culture." But, as a tool to help you scale a winning culture and avoid several of the most common culture traps, you want to have words that you can point to in order to communicate what you expect people to do. The startup entrepreneurs who were most successful in avoiding culture traps used *stories* to augment the words. Abby

Ross of ThinkCERCA, for example, has a file full of culture stories that she uses in her talks with new hires. So does Shradha Agarwal of Outcome Health. Rob Biederman, founder of Catalant Technologies provides another example of how important it is to capture stories:

> *When we hit 40 people, we knew that we had to define our culture. We had to document it, so we decided to come up with "cultural principles" that described how we worked and what was really important to us. At first, the founders did it over a dinner. Then we had an all-hands company meeting and people started to tell stories about what they called "our cool culture." From this meeting we took away 10 different themes that people had identified. Then we actually voted and five things popped out. It was the stories that made it all come alive for us.*

When Do You Document?

When is the best time to document a winning startup culture? In the beginning, startups are intimate. Everyone knows everyone. People's values and ambitions are on display. The founders interview and approve all new employees. The culture just *is*.

If the business grows and the startup is successful, there will come a point when the founders realize that the company's culture is an important source of competitive advantage, and they'd better not screw it up if they want to keep winning. So, they decide to document the culture and use the documentation to guide their future talent recruiting, to deal with employees who don't fit, and as a decision-making and enterprise-management tool as they scale the business. There is no perfect time to write it down, but here is what a bunch of successful entrepreneurs have to say about when to document a winning culture:

- Rob Biederman (see the above quote) did it when Catalant had 40 employees: "We didn't want there to be any mistake about what was important to us."

- Niraj Shah waited until Wayfair had to open new offices outside of its Boston headquarters: "Transferring our culture was a big deal, so we had to describe it in terms that others could relate to."

- Diane Hessan did it when she realized that her company's growth was starting to dilute Communispace's winning culture: "I was afraid that our new executives and managers would not understand how important our core values were and somehow our culture would break down."

- Rapid7's Corey Thomas believes that the time to institutionalize and document a winning culture is when you have multiple offices and have to give up personally screening every new hire: "You have to write it down when you have around 100 people and have to delegate the hiring decisions to others."

- Disruptor Beam's Jon Radoff found that culture became a critical success factor when the company scaled to the point when teams—rather than individual contributors—did the real work: "When we grew to 40 or 50 people, we started to be more disciplined about defining our culture. Now, after five years, we have decks, offsites, posters, and all sorts of documentation."

Shan Sinha, cofounder of Highfive, admitted that he waited too long to document his startup's culture, and he fell into the Taking Culture for Granted trap (Chapter 6). After selling his third company to Google in 2012, Sinha quickly raised $4 million and hired 10 high-powered engineers to work on Highfive's new video-conferencing software. He spent the first two years developing his product. "We cared about the culture, but didn't really describe or articulate it." In 2016, with over 50 people in the company, Highfive's newly hired head of marketing posted an edgy piece about Kellyanne Conway on the company's website in hopes of getting Donald Trump to tweet about it. According to Sinha:

All hell broke loose. Employees vociferously complained about the post and said 'this isn't me.' I was sent a Slack petition; some of the feedback was pretty nasty. The entire senior team spent 10 hours over a three-day period trying to figure out how to respond. We had always prided ourselves in having a freewheeling, risk-taking culture that valued ownership, but the reaction was a real wakeup call for me.

In an effort to, as he put it, "[R]ecast our cultural norms and clarify who we are," Sinha presented a Power Point deck to the entire company that recapped what had happened. Here is a partial sample of what the Power Point said:

Learnings

- The post was a calculated risk, not a lapse in judgment. Many agree that execution could be better ... But execution is not the issue here

- The deeply emotional internal reaction is a positive one. People care and associate their identities with Highfive

- We under-planned for handling interactions with customers, prospects, recruits, friends & team members

- We need to encourage, embrace & support **autonomous** risk taking

- Need to more clearly define our brand attributes & goals (which we suspect have become "too safe"/"boring")

- The "slack channel" and much of the ensuing feedback started in a good place and ended in a bad place

New Cultural Norms

- Embrace autonomous risk taking—across & within teams

- Question conventional wisdom

- Open debate is healthy

- Be thoughtful & assume others are equally so

Even entrepreneurs who have not yet documented their winning cultures, realize that it will become an important to-do if they want to avoid the culture traps described in Chapter 6.

- Richard Rabbat, founder of Gfycat, a two-year old startup, has yet to write it down: "When I was at Zynga, we had 7 Values that were widely publicized. I know that we'll have to document the Gfycat culture one day soon. We need a tool to help us hire the right kind of people. We need to tell job applicants what we're all about and what they're getting into, and we need to have a more explicit standard for all of our existing people."

- Alison Vercruysse, founder of 18 Rabbits, says: "Although our culture is a priority, we're too small to actually document it right now. We only have seven employees. Maybe when we grow to 10 or 12, we'll have to write it down . . . especially because I see us growing more as a virtual company, with people working out of their homes."

- Erez Nahom, founder of KonnecTo, expresses the same thought: "All of our engineers now are in the Tel Aviv office, but as soon as I move to New York and we start hiring in that office, we will have to document our cultural values and be more intentional about defining how we want to work together."

If you want to see the culture statements of successful startups that have documented and published them, take a look at Appendix A-3.

The 6 Characteristics of Successful Employees in Rapidly Growing Companies

Startup Institute, February 2015

Introduction

Our study and analysis of the responses of over 100 entrepreneurial leaders of rapidly growing companies has revealed a remarkably consistent set of 6 characteristics that successful employees possess. The pattern of knowledge, attitudes and skill uncovered in our research is supported by a number of academic studies, but this real-world validation provides insights for both would-be entrepreneurs and educators of this important population.

Background

A famous piece of advice, from the American business magnate, Warren Buffett, is that if your IQ is 150, you should sell 30 points to someone else. Buffett says that for most jobs, you only need to be "smart enough." When hiring, Buffett looks for intelligence, energy and integrity, and believes that "two out of three is not good enough."

One of the most successful airlines ever, Southwest, looks for "warriors" when they are hiring. Explains Sherry Phelps, their former head of employment: "So much of our history was born out of battles, fighting for the right to be an airline, fighting off the big guys who wanted to squash us, and now fighting off the low-cost airlines trying to emulate us. We are battle-born, battle-tried people. Anyone we add has to have some of that warrior spirit." (See Bill Taylor, <u>HBR</u>, "*Hire for Attitude, Train for Skill.*" <u>https://hbr.org/2011/02/hire-for-attitude-train-for-sk/</u>)

Executives from a wide range of both large and small companies have latched on to the notion that being smart and having a high level of technical skill is simply not enough to insure success. Many have even said that they would rather have a person of moderate skill with a great attitude than a technical whiz who lacks the right attitude and values.

We wondered how this point of view played out in startup and high-growth companies—where raw brainpower and technical competence would seem to be the keys to success. Digging a bit deeper, we wanted to identify the specific characteristics that executives of high-growth companies were looking for, and how these entrepreneurial leaders described their best employees.

In addition to fielding over 200 questionnaires, we also analyzed over 65 in-depth conversations with the executives of companies that are Startup Institute partners in Boston, Chicago, New York, London & Berlin.

Intellectual Horsepower and Technical Skills Are not Enough

The leaders of rapidly growing companies believe that technical genius and being "really smart" are poor predictors of success. These leaders told us that possessing what they often called "culture skills" was absolutely essential.

In fact, 92% of our respondents felt that soft skills were just as important as technical skills, and over 25% felt that they were more important.

This can be compared to a recent Career Builder survey, in which

77% of respondents said that soft and technical skills were equally important and where 16% felt that soft skills were more important. (http://www.careerbuilder.com/share/aboutus/pressreleasesdetail. aspx?sd=4/10/2014&id=pr817&ed=12/31/2014)1

It is clear that in the high-pressure world of companies that are starting up and scaling, the best employees are those who can do much more than the technical work.

They fit in with the team; they bring passion and a sense of possibility to the workplace; and they contribute to and help define the company's culture. Said one executive in a 400-person ad tech firm:

> *"More and more, I see that some of our brightest folks don't work out because they're awful to work with, incredibly stubborn, and don't evolve well."*

Or, from the CEO of a social media startup:

> *"We spend a lot of time together working days, night and weekends, and so if we aren't excited about the people we're in the trenches with, we're not going to get very far . . . We make sure we all get along, have a similar perspective on issues important to the company, and like to laugh together."*

Or the CEO of a London-based tech company:

> *"We believe that if someone has the right attitude* <u>and</u> *is talented, they will be able to figure out whatever challenge comes their way. Without the right attitude, the talent is wasted."*

Or from the leader of a Berlin 100-person startup:

> *"We can teach anything if the person is willing to work hard and learn. Our motto is EQ first and IQ second."*

So What Does Matter Most?

If intellectual horsepower and technical brilliance aren't enough, what does it take to succeed in a startup or rapidly scaling enterprise? Our research uncovered six critical characteristics that are the most highly valued by entrepreneurial leaders. These are the things that employers believe contribute the most to their company's growth and profitability:

1. *Desire to Learn*
2. *Ability to Thrive Amidst Ambiguity*
3. *Passion*
4. *Handling Setbacks with Scrappiness & Grit*
5. *Excellence at Collaboration*
6. *Willingness to put the Company before Oneself*

Desire to Learn

Most growth-company executives noted how fast everything is changing in their environment: their industries, their companies and their roles. As a result, the ability to listen and learn was judged to be critical skill. This was expressed in many ways: being curious, being coachable, having a "continuous improvement mindset", and being open to new ideas and approaches. Entrepreneurial leaders contrast such active learners with other employees who were smart and skilled technically, but believed they were smarter than everyone else and, therefore, less willing to listen to others and try new things. For example, in all too many tech startups, we heard of bright developers whose web development skills started to become obsolete and yet they resisted learning new languages.

Truly active learners realize that they don't know everything and have a "constant desire to get better." They are always looking for new ways of doing things and they are open to shifting their roles as the business changes. They are inquisitive, and as a result, they are viewed as "quick studies."

In our research, they were often described as "thinking fast on their feet." This means that they were willing to let go of positions and ideas that were not working and embrace new positions that seemed to have a greater chance of success.

Employees with a high desire to learn respond to feedback quite differently from others. They are not defensive; they frequently invite critical comments so they can "make it work better." They want to be an expert, but they realize that true expertise requires constantly learning new things. In our interviews, more than one executive commented that such employees have a special approach to learning that allows them to capture insights from disparate sources: personal experiences, teammates, teachers, readings, and even customers.

Finally, this desire to learn is more than just learning about the work or the business.

Outstanding employees were aware of their own faults and wanted to keep learning more about themselves. This quest for self-knowledge has long been cited as a critical component of "emotional intelligence" (EQ). (See Daniel Goleman http://www.amazon.com/ Emotional-Intelligence-Matter-More-Than/dp/055338371X#.)

Ability to Thrive Amidst Ambiguity

Companies that are starting up and scaling are nothing if not stressful. Uncertainty and ambiguity are everywhere. The last thing an entrepreneurial leader needs is an employee who panics when things are unknown or unclear. It is not surprising, then, that our research uncovered the high value placed on the ability to thrive in an ambiguous, high-stress environment.

One of the greatest sources of stress in rapidly growing companies is the lack of direction, the lack of clear marching orders, established procedures, or grooved processes. The best employees don't sit back and wait for someone to tell them what to do next. They create clarity when faced with confusion. They understand that there may not be someone to tell them what to do or how to do it. Almost every executive we spoke with talked about the need for self-starters: people who did not require constant oversight or direction, and who were not paralyzed in the midst of ambiguity and change. "Resourcefulness" and "resilience" were commonly used words; great people figure things out on their own, they are resourceful in a resource-constrained environment, and their ability to thrive in such a world tends to resonate throughout the organization.

"We love people who are cool cucumbers when the shit hits the fan," remarked one startup CEO. We heard countless stories of the person who came into an unclear and directionless situation, figured everything out on her own, stayed calm under pressure, and operated without undue drama or panic.

What is behind this characteristic? The executives in our survey believed that it was a combination of having personal strength and business acumen. Outstanding employees seem to have figured out how their companies operate, and thus they know how to connect the dots to produce results that matter most, especially when "the shit hits the fan." These highly valued people, therefore, are able to rise above the inherent ambiguity in high-growth work environments. They tend to see the big picture, and, as one executive said, "they don't sweat the small stuff." They keep their knees bent, accepting that things will be ambiguous and they are constantly on the lookout for new ways of doing things.

Passion

In our research, the leaders of fast-growing companies placed a high value on passion—and they described their most valuable employees as those who gladly and consistently put in the time and dedication to make their companies a success. Not surprisingly, they had plenty of terms for those who didn't: clock-watchers, whiners, and not-my-jobbers. The best employees raise their hands, pitch in everywhere, and do anything that is needed to move the company forward. They seem to have proactivity and passion in their veins.

The notion of high levels of motivation and a strong work ethic has always been important to employers. But we uncovered a slightly broader source of such "passion for work." What is valued most in startups and high-growth companies is passion that is less about "I work hard because hard work is a good thing", and more about "I work hard because I love my job and I am proud of this company, and I will gladly pick up more if I can help it achieve its mission." This kind of passion leads to a high-energy, "let's-make-it-happen" work environment. Because of the uncertainty and lack of resources, it's not always very pretty, but it sure is action-packed. That's a tradeoff the executives in our study would gladly make.

The kind of passion and motivation that executives in our survey valued the most had another important dimension, which was the presence of high personal standards. Several of our entrepreneurial leaders said that their favorite employees had "high ambitions for the business." But they also talked about the importance of having people who understood the limits to these ambitions—the need for personal integrity, for not cutting corners and the commitment to excellence, even if that meant spending a bit more time or money to "get it right." As one executive put it:

> *"I need to trust that my people will not let their passion compromise our values or blind them to doing what's right—for our business, our customers and our owners."*

Handling Setbacks with Scrappiness and Grit

Growth-company executives place a very high premium on employees who are scrappy—who don't get bogged down in process and instead who can face setbacks and difficult situations and still move forward. The best employees, even when confronted with tasks they had never done before, are doers. They are persistent and have the temperament and desire to "see it through," even when old assumptions prove to be wrong. Scrappiness means "learning by doing:" taking small steps and evaluating what's going right and what's going wrong before committing the firm's limited resources to a course of action.

Even when things go wrong, they have grit: the persistence to keep digging in, pushing ahead, making do with the resources at hand, being tough and believing that taking personal responsibility is the right strategy. This doesn't always work in larger, more established organizations, with their checks and balances and budgets and control systems. But in startups and high-growth business environments this approach to handling setbacks turns out to be one of the keys to success.

Taken together, scrappiness and grit allow fast growing companies to overcome their limited resources. As one CEO told us:

> *Our most successful people are focused on how to make things happen rather than the reasons why things cannot happen. This can-do attitude is essential in our kind of company. . . . These people act like they are masters of their own destiny.*

The most valued employees have a self-confidence that allows them to accept setbacks and keep moving forward without being overly cautious or paralyzed by a fear of failure. Len Schlesinger and Charles Kiefer have written about this characteristic in their book, Action Trumps Everything. The authors note that detailed analysis and planning work well for businesses with lots of clarity and certainty.On the other hand, when the rules and goals are constantly shifting, people have no choice but to act without perfect information. When dealing with inevitable setbacks, small steps forward (what we call being scrappy) trump hesitation and cautiousness.

Handling Setbacks with Scrappiness and Grit is closely related to the Ability to Thrive Amidst Ambiguity. However, "thriving" is more a matter of creating clarity, of keeping the big picture in mind and of staying calm when others are stressed out. Scrappiness and Grit is more about how great people get results, about how they move forward when things go wrong, how they respond to setbacks by taking small steps—what Schlesinger and Kiefer call "the right kind of action."

Excellence at Collaboration

Our study found that the most valued employees appreciate the contributions of others and have the ability to work with a team to get the job done. For these people, their job motivation is less about individual glory and more about being an active part of a cohesive and powerful team.

Excellence at collaboration requires a varied set of interpersonal and communication skills. Executives of high-growth companies reported that strong collaborators speak up in meetings, but don't drown out others. They contribute, but know they don't have all the answers. They help those around them become better, and they trust that others will do the same for them. They know how to get information and buy-in from others, but they don't get bogged down with endless conversations. They are confident, but act without ego. Truly outstanding collaborators make significant contributions to corporate culture by publically recognizing others for hard work and sincerely appreciating the collective talents of the organization.

Very often, executives chided their precocious and technically savvy employees who lacked collaborative instincts. It became clear to us that their best employees combined brains and a drive for results with the ability to build healthy and productive collaborative relationships. As the CEO of a fast-growing consumer brand told us, they are "hard on problems, but not on people."

Finally, when asked about how they experienced good collaboration, executives painted vivid pictures of employees laughing, patting each other on the back, drawing pictures together, sharing stories, and of eating pizza with their teams.

Willingness to Put the Company Before Oneself

The executives in our study told countless stories of not-so-valued employees who were completely focused on themselves: frequently asking for promotions, worried about how everything affects them, and overly focused on title and position. In contrast, the best employees consistently seemed to put the company first, making decisions with the interests of the business in mind.

This characteristic was more than not being self-centered. It was the desire to be part of something bigger than themselves, excited about the company and the opportunity to contribute in a meaningful way. A frequently used word was "ownership," in the sense that the most valued employees act as if they are major shareholders of the enterprise. When combined with being a self-starter and a healthy dose of passion, these employees would never think to ask "who is going to take care of this for me?"

In a very real sense, the employees who were valued the most were the ones that "fell in love" with the company's mission. Falling in love means understanding and believing in the business—not only the part of the business he/she is working on, but also the grand purpose of the enterprise as a whole. This perspective and commitment to the enterprise is an important culture-building characteristic, highly valued by the executives in our survey.

The Willingness to Put the Company Before Oneself helps explain one of the sources of our third characteristic, Passion. However, our sixth characteristic is different. It is focused less on energy level and motivation and more on attitude and perspective. The difference may be clearer by examining the lack of each characteristic. A lack of Passion is associated with an unwillingness to work the extraordinary hours often required in a startup. A lack of passion means a lack of achievement motivation, and an absence of a "hey, let's make it happen" enthusiasm. On the other hand, a lack of the ability to put the company first is associated with a more traditional focus on career advancement, a "me first" attitude, and a certain narrowness of purpose. (By the way, this can be coupled with lots of hard work.)

A Final Thought About the 6 Characteristics

It should be noted that none of the six characteristics we have described is sufficient to be a singular differentiator. Almost all of the executives we interviewed cited at least three of the characteristics, and none believed that there was only one factor that made all the difference. Therefore, we believe that the six should be viewed as a powerful "success cluster." Because we did not know before hand what aptitudes or skills would be identified as critical, we can only hypothesize that they are largely complementary.

For example, it may be easy to imagine that the employee who exhibits a high degree of Scrappiness and Grit also has the ability to Thrive Amidst Ambiguity & Setbacks. This same employee probably has a good degree of Passion, and perhaps, a strong Desire to Learn. As researchers, it is less clear that Excellence at Collaboration and the Willingness to Put the Company Before Oneself—which were often mentioned together by our respondents—are quite as complementary with the first four. Although they seem to stand more by themselves, they also were viewed as two of the most valued.

Implications

In this age of technology and innovation, clearly companies need smart people who are skilled in relevant fields. Web developers, Internet security experts, UX designers, and data managers are all in high demand. So are expert salespeople and marketers who understand the new world of HTML, CSS, SEO, data, and Google analytics. However, in the eyes of the executives in charge of high-growth companies—from CEOs to VPs of Recruiting—technical skills are far from sufficient for employee success. The best people have skills, attitudes and mindsets that differentiate them from other high-powered recruits. If they can be spotted and hired, they will help entrepreneurial leaders build strong, high performing companies with truly great cultures.

These differentiating attributes and characteristics are not always sought or taught at the university level. Quite frankly, not all of them are easily identifiable or teachable.

At Startup Institute, we accept 25% of our applicants, and we look very hard at the six characteristics in our evaluation of candidates. Every candidate is interviewed, re-interviewed, given trial assignments, and assessed by our admissions team to ensure that we have the right raw material.

Once candidates pass these mindset and behavioral screens, they learn technical skills in their specific track—and, in parallel, our core curriculum focuses on these same six characteristics that our sponsors and others deemed to be the keys to success. Students are put in unclear situations where they have to figure things out, they work intensively and in teams, they learn to act instead of over-processing, and they learn to push forward in the face of ambiguity, setbacks and uncertainty. Their passions are defined and refined. And, our alumni continually send us examples from their work experiences that reinforce the importance of the culture-building skills we develop.

Finally, although we studied companies that were starting out and rapidly scaling, it's no secret that even large organizations are expressing the same need for the kinds of well-rounded entrepreneurial behaviors that we have uncovered in this research. The more that change, innovation, uncertainty and the need for teamwork define the workplace of the future, the greater the need will be for people who thrive and succeed in this kind of environment.

Endnotes

Introduction

[1] Hemerling, Jim, and Julie Kilmann. 2013. "High-Performance Culture: Getting It, Keeping It." *BCG Perspectives*. At https:// www.bcgperspectives.com/content/articles/engagement_culture_ people_management_human_resources_high_performance_ culture_getting_it_keeping_it/

[2] Schein, Edgar H. 1985. *Organizational Culture and Leadership*. San Francisco, CA.: Jossey-Bass.

[3] Schneider, Benjamin. 1990. *Organizational Climate and Culture*. San Francisco, CA.: Jossey-Bass.

Chapter 2

[1] Thiel, Peter. 2014. *Zero to One*. New York: Crown Business.124.

[2,3] Kim, Jungsoo, and Richard de Dear. 2013. "Workspace satisfaction: The privacy-communication trade-off in open-plan offices." *Journal of Environmental Psychology* (December) 36: 18–26. At https://doi.org/10.1016/j.jenvp.2013.06.007. Kaufman, Lindsey. 2014. "Google got it wrong. The open-office trend is destroying the workplace." *The Washington Post*. At https://www.washingtonpost. com/posteverything/wp/2014/12/30/google-got-it-wrong- the-open-office-trend-is-destroying-the-workplace/?utm_ term=.89c83919826e.

Chapter 3

[1] https://www.recode.net/2017/11/7/16617340/read-uber-dara-khosrowshahi-new-rule-values-meeting

[2] https://www.linkedin.com/pulse/ubers-new-cultural-norms-dara-khosrowshahi/

[3] Manjoo, Farhad. 2017. "Uber's Lesson: Silicon Valley's Start-Up Machine Needs Fixing." *The New York Times.* "Technology." June 21. At https://www.nytimes.com/2017/06/21/technology/uber-start-up-lessons.html.

[4] della Cava, Marco, and Kevin McCoy. 2017. "Bro Culture Is Under Attack, But Women Say it's far from Tamed." USA Today. August 21. https://www.usatoday.com/story/money/2017/08/21/bro-culture-under-attack-but-women-say-its-far-tamed/559005001/

Chapter 4

[1] Thiel, Peter. 2014. *Zero to One.* New York: Crown Business.109.

[2] Horowitz, Ben. 2014. *The Hard Thing About Hard Things: Building a Business When There Are No Easy Answers..* New York: Harper Business. 180.

[3] Thiel, Peter. 2014. *Zero to One.* New York: Crown Business.123–4.

[4] Lyons, Dan. 2016. *Disrupted.* Boston: Hachette Books. 74-5.

[5] Thiel, Peter. 2014. *Zero to One.* New York: Crown Business.124–5.

[6] Wasserman, Noam. 2012. *The Founder's Dilemmas.* Princeton: Princeton University Press. 96.

Appendix A

[1] Schein, Edgar H. 1999. *The Corporate Culture Survival Guide*. San Francisco: Jossey-Bass.

[2] Litwin, George, and Robert Stringer. 1968. *Motivation and Organizational Climate* Cambridge: Harvard University Press.

[3] Litwin, George, and Robert Stringer, The Forum Corporation (training manual (1975). Boston: The Forum Corporation

[4] Stringer, Robert. 2002. Leadership and Organizational Climate. Upper Saddle River, NJ: Prentice Hall. 46–51.

[5] Litwin, George, and Robert Stringer. 1968. *Motivation and Organizational Climate* Cambridge: Harvard University Press.189.

Acknowledgments

Writing this book has been the most rewarding professional experience of my life. It allowed me to reflect on all the academic research and work that I've done over the past several decades, and to apply it to the work I'm doing currently—coaching, mentoring, and investing in startup businesses.

I couldn't have written *Culture.com: How the Best Startups Make it Happen* without the help and assistance of Kate Merritt, my longtime colleague, business partner, and fellow researcher. Kate and I conducted the majority of the interviews with entrepreneurs in 2017, and we collaborated on the intellectual framework for every chapter of the book.

In addition to Kate, my brother, David Stringer provided me with invaluable feedback when he reviewed the original draft of the manuscript as we worked together during a getaway week in Scottsdale. And Alison Lowander, editor extraordinaire, helped to craft the final version of this book.

My journey into the world of human motivation and my appreciation of the enormous impact that culture has on people's day-to-day behavior started with my first mentor, Dr. George Litwin. The ideas that George led me to explore at Harvard are even more powerful today than they were when we were engaged in our original research.

As a former consultant, VC, business-school professor, and seed capital investor, I have learned a boatload about organizations large and small, and most recently, about startups. My initial work in this area was influenced by enlightening conversations with Jan Bruce of meQuilibrium, Caroline Freedman of Freed Foods, Sebastian Martin of Cambio Coffee, Katie Bickford of Starry, Jen Faigel of Commonwealth Kitchen, Jeremy Halpern of Nutter McClennen & Fish, Charles Trevail, Jessica DeVlieger, Corey Schwartz, Manila Austin, Bill Alberti and others at C Space, JB Kassarjian, Keith Rollag, Tom Simon, and Phyllis Schlesinger of Babson, Len Schlesinger at HBS, Dave McLaughlin at Vsnap and WeWork, Jennie Ripps and Maria Littlefield of Wise Owl Holdings, Kevin McGovern of The Water Initiative, Chris Sinclair of Mattel, Ben Jabbawy of Privy, Jean Hammond of Learn Launch, Zac Sheffer of Elsen, Jeremy Au of CozyKin, Dave Balter of BzzAgent, Smarterer, and Flipside Crypto, and Tom Cates of Sales Equity.

Perhaps the most important people to thank and acknowledge are all the entrepreneurs who gave us their valuable time so that we could learn what winning startup cultures looked and felt like—and how these cultures were created and successfully scaled. Almost all my research interviews were conducted in person. Several were Skype interviews or long distance phone calls. All were fascinating and informative.

My East Coast collaborators were Joshua Summers of clypd, Rob Biederman of Catalant, Bob Gett of Viant, Katie Burke of HubSpot, Ellen Rubin of Clear Sky Data, Niraj Shah of Wayfair, Scott Savitz of Shoebuy and Data Point Capital, Stefania Mallett of ezCater, Gail Goodman of Constant Contact, Tom Dretler of Shorelight Education, Fred Shilmover of Insight Squared, Corey Thomas of Rapid7, Jon Radoff of Disruptor Beam, T.J. Mahony of FlipKey and Accomplice, Brent Grinna of EverTrue, Bettina Hein of Pixability, Eric Paley of Founder Collective, Greg Besner of Culture IQ, Janet Kraus of Peach, Rich DiTieri of Startup Institute, Havell Rodrigues of Adjoint, Adam O'Neal of Broga, Tryg Siverson and Vanessa Phillips of Feel Good Foods, Jim King of GaGa's, Bob Jones of Scientific Nutrition Products, David Morris of Smart Lunches, Mike Tardiff of Sourcetop, Jules Pieri of The Grommet, Jon Davis of The Davis Companies, David McCue of McCue Corp, Jordan Fliegel of Draft, John Kelley of CoachUp and David Friedman of Boston Logic.

My Midwest and California collaborators were Alison Vercruysse of 18 Rabbits, Anthony Rodio of Your Mechanic, Shan Sinha of High Five, Richard Rabbat of Gfycat, Conor Begley of Tribe Dynamics, Dan Chao of Halo Neuroscience, Christian Selchau-Hansen and Mike Tamir at Takt, Ron Croen of You & Mr Jones, Greg Gollub, and Di Cullen at Sequoia, Mandy Yoh of ReviewTrackers, Canh Tran of Rippleshot, Melissa Footlick of TopStepTrader, Abby Ross of ThinkCERCA, Shradha Agarwal of Outcome Health, Shaunt Sarkissian of Cortex, Alex Bayer of Genius Juice, Mike Brungardt of Pro Hoop Strength, Jim Hummer of Whole Health, and Tony Hsieh of Zappos.

Collaborators who founded startups outside the US include Furquan Kidwai of Enabling Healthologies in Pakistan), Eran Gronich of Flying Spark, Ltd., in Israel, Michalis Gkontas of FORKY in Greece, Tomas Froes of Frostimo, in China, Erez Nahom of KonnecTo in Israel, Franco Capurro of One Key Ventures & Caaapital in Chile and Mexico, and David Thorrold of BioVittoria, in New Zealand & China.

Finally, I have to acknowledge the tremendous encouragement and support of Diane Hessan, my entrepreneurial partner and wife. Not only did Diane introduce me to her broad network of VCs, founders, and startup companies, but her personal business experiences also formed the foundation of many of the lessons learned about how the best startups make winning cultures happen.

Index

Made in the USA
Middletown, DE
29 May 2021